A TOUCH OF LOVE

A Touch of Love

JOHN & JANET HOUGHTON

KINGSWAY PUBLICATIONS
EASTBOURNE

ISBN 0 86065 461 3

Unless otherwise indicated, biblical quotations are from
the New International Version, © New York International
Bible Society 1978.

RSV = Revised Standard Version
copyrighted 1946, 1952, © 1971, 1973 by the
Division of Christian Education of the National
Council of the Churches of Christ in the USA

Front cover photo: Tony Stone Photolibrary—London

Printed in Great Britain for
KINGSWAY PUBLICATIONS LTD
1 St Anne's Road, Eastbourne, E. Sussex BN21 3UN by
Clays Ltd, St Ives plc
Typeset by Nuprint Services Ltd, Harpenden, Herts

With thanks to the One
whose touch
gave us love

O that you would kiss me with the kisses of your mouth!

Woman to Man (Song of Solomon 1:2, RSV)

Let thy fountain be blessed: and rejoice with the wife of thy youth. Let her be as the loving hind and pleasant roe; let her breasts satisfy thee at all times; and be thou ravished always with her love.

(Proverbs 5:18–19, AV)

Contents

Note: while always appreciating letters of encouragement, the authors regret that they are unable to enter into correspondence concerning readers' personal problems.

Introduction

Almost everybody wants a satisfying love-life. Unfortunately, very few seem to find one. We live in a world of sexual freedom without fulfilment, of technique without trust, of expectation without endeavour. Not surprisingly, in a society which divorces sexual experience from loving commitment we find many who started out with high hopes now drowning in the disillusionment of a broken marriage and wondering where on earth they went wrong.

But it needn't be like that at all. It's perfectly possible to enjoy a marriage in which profound sexual satisfaction is combined with passionate romance and life-long faithfulness. This book springs from that conviction.

As you would expect in what is essentially a sex manual, the following pages contain explicit and medically accurate information upon all aspects of sexual intercourse. But making love is much more than just a half-hour scientific technique. It's the supreme expression of a deep and tender passion between two lovers. This is a very human matter involving all our feelings. Hence, you'll find we've also included quite a lot about relationship building along the way. This accounts too for us adopting a personal and somewhat informal style of writing. We believe a sex manual should be 'user friendly'.

For convenience, we've grouped the material under five major themes: Engagement, the Honeymoon, The Art of Love-Making, Having Children and A Lifetime of Love. As such, the book is ideally suited to those who are just setting out on the road and who desire a map for the journey. However, it is also intended for couples who have travelled some distance and who wish to take their bearings by referring to the sections appropriate to them. Some may, in any case, want to read the earlier parts in order to review their progress, especially if they feel they've wandered a bit off course.

Although sexually experienced readers will inevitably find some things 'old hat', it is a fact that many people still approach marriage with a mixture of naivety and popular misconceptions. We'd be performing a disservice to such folk if we didn't spell out what may be patently obvious to others. So please bear with us.

We've written this book as lovers ourselves and also as committed Christians. Some may think this a contradiction. How can you be a Christian and enjoy sex? This is a common fallacy. Far from being opposed to sexual pleasure, those who know and trust in the Lord Jesus Christ are actually some of the best at relishing it. Only a lifeless religion would frown upon such a good gift from God!

You may or may not share our convictions. Either way, we hope our book will help you to make love without shame, fear or frustration—and to discover that biblical moral values, far from being restrictive, are the most truly liberating of all.

Finally, we are deeply indebted to the many folk who have trustingly shared their experiences with us over the years and so enabled us to see things more clearly. We are particularly grateful to Dr John Carey FRCGP, DRCOG, for his generous and perceptive observations which have contributed much to the accuracy of the text and to Dr David Guckenheim MB, BS, who gave help on the sexually transmitted diseases. To all these friends we offer our thanks. Any shortcomings in the final result are entirely our own responsibility.

JOHN & JANET HOUGHTON

ENGAGEMENT

This opening section is addressed to engaged couples who wish to know how best to conduct the physical side of their relationship during the months leading up to their marriage. It also contains a non-technical guide to 'the facts of life' together with practical information about birth control.

I

A Shortage of Virgins

Poets write about it; minstrels sing. Maidens pine and grown men sigh. Battles are fought, blood is shed, kingdoms change hands. For no price is too high in the pursuit of love.

It's a lot less dramatic than that for most of us. We're neither knights in shining armour nor damsels in distress; just ordinary people living in the late twentieth century. But for all that, when we fall in love we still experience something of the power of that romantic passion which drove the legendary heroes of the past. For there's nothing quite like this sexual attraction between a man and a woman. It preoccupies and entices us until every part of our being yearns for our loved one and we know we cannot live separate lives any longer. We must get married. Or, at least, share a common bed.

This latter option is a reminder that sexual values have undergone radical changes during the past few decades. No longer do most people wait until marriage before indulging in sexual intercourse; few are virgins on their wedding night. Whereas marriage once marked the commencement of intimacies, nowadays, if it takes place at all, it's only an agreement to restrict them to one partner. Soaring divorce figures suggest that many don't keep their word even in this.

The old Christian standards seem far removed from a society in which almost anything goes—a remnant of an ancient religion suited only to repressed traditionalists who are too scared to do otherwise. Typical of this view was a television debate which we watched some years ago. The topic was 'Lust' and a well-known actor set out to defend its virtue by equating it with passion. A Salvation Army captain argued against lust because he equated it with sexual desire outside of wedlock. This confusion left the actor appearing passionately immoral and the Salvationist virtuous but dull. The audience preferred the passion to the purity.

But that either/or conclusion is based upon a misunderstanding of what the Bible actually teaches about sex and marriage. So, before we go any further, we feel it only fair to clarify just what Christians do believe on the subject. Whether you wish to accept this view or not is a matter for your own conscience but we trust you'll at least find it helpful to consider the option.

*   *   *

We'd like to begin by briefly comparing two sorts of love. One kind comes from God; the other is mankind's own creation.

God is Love in person, so we know that when he expresses his love it's going to have very special qualities. We can sum these up in the term *covenant love*—an expression which is used to convey a sense of total commitment, lifelong faithfulness and sacrificial devotion towards the one on the receiving end. All this was vividly demonstrated in God's sacrifice of his own Son, Jesus, for our sins. 'This is how we know what love is: Jesus Christ laid down his life for us' (1 John 3:16).

Covenant love involves giving your word that you'll never go back on your commitment to give all that you are to the one you love. That's what Christian marriage means and it reflects the very heart of God. In fact, he uses the wedding image to describe his own loyalty towards his people:

> I looked at you and saw that you were old enough for love ... I
> gave you my solemn oath and entered into a covenant with

you, declares the Sovereign Lord, and you became mine (Ezekiel 16:8).

Never will I leave you; never will I forsake you (Hebrews 13:5).

Sexual intercourse belongs only within the bounds of covenant love. The joining of our bodies is designed to express the joining of our lives. If that hasn't taken place then not only does sex lose much of its meaning but it becomes dishonest into the bargain. We say that we're one by our actions, but our lives deny it. That's hypocrisy.

There's another factor to be taken into consideration. If we're creatures made in the image of God, our behaviour should mirror his character, that is, reflect his glory. By having sexual intercourse outside of marriage we actually contradict something fundamental about the nature of God —his covenant love. Instead of demonstrating his glory we deny it. We 'unworship' him—and that is sin.

It's not surprising then to find the scriptures teaching that sex outside of marriage is the sin of immorality. The will of God is chastity for single people and absolute fidelity for the married. Hebrews 13:4 says, 'Marriage should be honoured by all, and the marriage bed kept pure, for God will judge the adulterer and all the sexually immoral.' Jesus applied this to our attitudes as well as our actions: 'Anyone who looks at a woman lustfully has already committed adultery with her in his heart' (Matthew 5:28).

The reason many find this hard to accept nowadays is because our society has adopted another kind of love. Instead of being about deep commitment it's about feelings and pleasurable experiences, especially sexual ones. This 'love' has been made into a new god, though it's really only the old god of self-gratification in disguise.

The result is that love has come to mean little more than sex for many folk today. So we have people sleeping around, casual sex, sex outside of marriage, homosexuality, adultery and so on—all in the name of love. We've become obsessed with techniques for maximum physical satisfaction, but without concentrating on how to build good relationships. Sex education has been divorced from marriage in our schools. Courting couples consider that by having sex they're expressing love for one another. The promiscuous student is 'an experienced lover'. Adultery is justified as 'falling in love' and we're all supposed to be 'mature' about it.

For the chasing after this new god our society is prepared to abort its children, break its hearts, ruin its homes and wreck its future. To our mind it's a high price to pay for a poor, pale mimic of the real thing. 'Love' it may be called but it's certainly not from God.

So, what are we to do? Indulge our passions at will, satisfy the hunger on demand in whatever way suits us best? Or opt for God's covenant love?

The objection often raised to Christian marriage is that it's no more than a correct but miserable duty to please a harsh God. To take this path must surely mean developing a cold, 'spiritual' relationship with our partner and woe betide us if we feel anything like passion for one another. After all the apostle Paul wrote:

> This is the will of God, your sanctification: that you abstain from immorality; that each one of you know how to take a wife for himself in holiness and honour, not in the passion of lust like heathen who do not know God (1 Thessalonians 4:3–5, RSV).

There certainly are Christians who have understood it that way and taught that intercourse is solely for having children and not for pleasure. In fact, we came across this quite recently in France of all places. Some French believers were teaching that birth control was wrong, yet if a couple had too many children they were obviously having too much sex, maybe even enjoying it, so they must be unspiritual!

You'll perhaps be relieved to know that this is not actually what God's word teaches. There's a world of difference between 'the passion of lust' to which Paul refers and the passion of love. The one is selfish and based purely upon an animal desire for sex; the other is an ardent, caring heart towards a complete person. That kind of sexual desire for one's married partner is a good and right thing. In fact, so much so that God included a book in the Bible which is wholly occupied with the passionate sexual love of a young married couple. It's called the Song of Songs and here are a few examples of their feelings. You may like to read the whole poem at some time as we'll be referring to it on several occasions throughout this book.

Beloved: Let him kiss me with the kisses of his mouth—for your love is more delightful than wine.

Lover: How beautiful you are, my darling! Oh, how beautiful.

Beloved: How handsome you are, my lover! Oh, how charming! And our bed is verdant... I am faint with love.

Lover: You have stolen my heart, my sister, my bride; you have stolen my heart with one glance of your eyes... Turn your eyes from me; they overwhelm me.

Beloved: I belong to my lover, and his desire is for me... for love is as strong as death, its jealousy unyielding as the grave. It burns like blazing fire, like a mighty flame (Song of Songs 1:2, 15, 16; 2:5; 4:9; 6:5; 7:10; 8:6).

Heady stuff and all in the Bible! God isn't opposed to sexual pleasure. He invented it! No one need fear that covenant love means no fun or feelings.

*   *   *

From this point on we're going to assume that you and your partner are either committed Christians or at least sympathetic to a Christian view of sex and marriage. This being the case, you may have been wrestling with an uncomfortable question ever since you started reading this book. It's this: what about if you've done it all already?

Either or both of you may have had previous sexual experience. You may be having sexual intercourse together at present or be masturbating one another to orgasm, or at least to a high degree of sexual arousal.

Possibly one or other of you has slept around in your pre-Christian days or at least been sexually intimate with someone else. Sadly, this may even have happened since your conversion.

Your questions may run like this: how do we get into the will of God from where we are? Is it too late? Is it even right for us to marry now? Or: we're in love and our intercourse is a true expression of that. Should we stop? How can we?

Putting matters right

If you're going to enter the blessings of the Lord's covenant love you must first bring your immoral love to an end. A new love-life in the will of God can only arise if the old is dead and buried. 'Put to death, therefore, whatever belongs to your earthly nature: sexual immorality, impurity, lust, evil desires and greed, which is idolatry' (Colossians 3:5).

What are the practical steps towards doing this?

We'll assume you've been having intercourse together. It may be because all your relationships have been like that or you may just have gone too far as a previously chaste couple. You may or may not feel very guilty about it. That's not really the point. This is a matter of spiritual obedience for you both rather than an issue of your feelings.

Your first step of repentance must be to stop having intercourse together until you are married. It won't be easy. Once sexual desire is awakened it doesn't go back to sleep. You've been used to each other's warmth and passion. You've enjoyed pleasure. It's now a habitual part of your relationship.

You'll help one another greatly if you agree about this together before God. We also want to suggest you tell your pastor about it. Hopefully, he won't throw you out of the church but will pray for you to have strength to do the will of God. You may feel scared of telling him what's been going on, but it will help you if you can. 'Confess your sins to each other and pray for each other so that you may be healed' (James 5:16). The Lord can use this to heal the inadequateness of your relationship.

For a little while it will feel as though you don't love each other any more. Gone are the intimacies of body, the caresses, the passion. This is the most difficult part to handle and is a kind of sexual burial phase in your relationship. That doesn't mean it's a fruitless time. Jesus went to his own grave knowing his Father would raise him up to newness of life. Have faith that God will raise up a far more glorious love-life than the one you put to death.

This is the time to deepen and fill out your relationship. Talk a lot. Seek to discover each other as real friends. One of the problems with sex before marriage is that it short-circuits the development of your relationship. Some parts of your circuitry remain dead as it were. Now is the opportunity to light up your emotional, spiritual and intellectual life together. It may seem hard at first but you'll be the richer for it.

Talk out your feelings of frustration, the oddness of setting limits. We've some practical advice about the kind of physical affection which will help you in the next chapter. Above all, trust God. He's restoring a virginity of heart to you both. The seeds of a God-given sexual love are being planted. Soon the green shoot of a wonderful new love will spear through the soil of your hearts and you'll be full of the joyful anticipation of celebrating that on your wedding night.

Other lovers

Let's move on to consider another common problem. Supposing you've had other lovers in the past? You may feel quite guilty about this. What if your partner finds out? If he thinks you're still a virgin, and you aren't, will he still want you? Should you tell him the truth?

The Bible says,

> If we walk in the light, as he is in the light, we have fellowship
> with one another, and the blood of Jesus, his Son, purifies us
> from all sin (1 John 1:7).

The truth will draw you closer. Choose a moment when
you're at ease with one another and you've plenty of time.
Then share it. 'I've something to tell you, darling. It's not
very easy to talk about, but I must 'cos I love you and I don't
want any secrets between us....'

If you find yourself on the receiving end of such a confession
we hope you'll realize how very difficult it really is for your
fiancée and instead of being hurt and affronted you'll find
love and respect welling up in your heart towards this brave
and beautiful girl. Thank her for telling you and assure her it
makes no difference to your love for her. Indeed, her honesty
deepens it. And you may well have some things you need to
confess as well. In fact, it might be you who needs to initiate
this particular conversation, in any case.

Incidentally, if either of you has been quite promiscuous in
the past and perhaps had several sexual partners you might
have picked up what the prophet Hosea calls 'a spirit of
prostitution' (Hosea 4:12). This may or may not be an actual
demon but it would be helpful to seek counsel from your
spiritual advisors and to receive whatever ministry they
consider appropriate.

Most young couples can cope with the knowledge that
their partner has been intimate with others in the past,
provided they feel sure of faithfulness now. But it can be a
very different matter if one of you has to confess to
homosexual inclinations or experience. It raises the question
as to whether you are going to be able to make it together as a
man and woman. How do you handle this one?

It must be confessed, of course. You owe that to your
intended. But how the disclosure is received is of the utmost
importance. If your fiancé has had homosexual involvement

in the past don't try to check that he's normal now by seducing him! Most homosexual problems arise because of a dominant mother/weak father syndrome. Come on strong and you'll frighten him off. He needs a very gentle and reassuring woman, someone whom he can trust and in whom he can find security.

Similarly, if your fiancée has had experience with other women it's no use acting the macho part. Your sacrificial tenderness is what she really needs. You must woo her and treat her as a full woman. A lack of men treating her properly in the past may well have initiated the problem.

If these have been your difficulties, we do recommend you take some counsel from your spiritual leaders or a trusted mature friend. Now is the time to sort it all out.

Sexually transmitted diseases

One other matter concerns us in this chapter. If you've been promiscuous in the past you may have picked up some disease and fear passing it on to your partner. In fact, now that you've found real love you might be afraid that it's all going to be ruined. You think you're being punished for your past sin. And if you confess that you're sexually diseased, well....

Unfortunately, because of widespread immorality, sexually transmitted diseases are becoming quite common. The most vulnerable people are those who've had multiple partners, though a disease may be contracted from just one other person. If you've not had intercourse or other close sexual involvement before then your chances of having picked something up are virtually zero. Worriers take note!

Certain parts of our bodies, including our mouths and some areas of our sexual organs, are lined with what are called mucous membranes. These moist surfaces are not only more vulnerable to damage than other parts but may also allow germs into the bloodstream. This is how sexually transmitted diseases are generally passed on.

Of course, just as our mouths get all sorts of passing complaints which are not too serious, so do our sexual organs. Most infections pass in a few days. If they don't then medical treatment is advisable. The majority of these problems are not caused by sexual intercourse.

To help you check out, we've included a simple list of the main complaints in Appendix One. If you honestly think you have a venereal disease then look up the nearest clinic in a telephone directory under Venereal Diseases. These are often called Special Clinics and are attached to main hospitals. The clinics are far more concerned about halting the spread of disease than judging your morals, so don't be afraid to go along.

If you think you have a non-venereal complaint then visit your local GP who will usually be able to advise you and prescribe a simple effective remedy. Above all, don't panic!

*   *   *

If you've read this chapter and it doesn't apply to you because you're on clear ground, praise God. We've written it for all those folk who sincerely want to do the will of God, who have perhaps only recently been converted, yet who remember all too painfully their sinful past. We hope our counsel will help.

God is a God of hope. He forgives, he restores, he makes new. That's the wonder of the Christian message; a truly clean sheet and a fresh start full of the Holy Spirit and with Jesus in charge.

King David made a real mess of his sex life when he took Bathsheba. He later confessed his sin to God. Psalm 51 is the record and here's part of it.

> Create in me a pure heart, O God, and renew a steadfast spirit within me. Do not cast me from your presence or take your Holy Spirit from me. Restore to me the joy of your salvation and grant me a willing spirit, to sustain me (Psalm 51:10–12).

God heard David and he'll hear you too if you honestly want to be forgiven. As you come into his will, he'll lead you into a pure and passionate sexual fulfilment together. It will be just as if you'd never sinned.

2

How Far Should We Go?

They sat for what seemed an eternity, staring silently at the magic of the moonlit sea. He had his arm about her and she could feel him trembling slightly. She squeezed his hand reassuringly. This was the moment they had been anticipating for weeks.

He turned to face her. She smiled encouragement as he looked deep into her dark brown eyes. When he spoke his voice, though soft, was earnest.

'Darling, I love you so much. Let's always be together,' he whispered. 'Please, will you marry me?'

It was what she had longed to hear from the moment they had fallen in love. She flung her arms around his neck.

'Oh, yes, darling,' she cried. 'Yes, I will!'

Yours may not have been the 'magic of the moonlit sea' version. It could have taken place in a restaurant, on a park bench, in the front room or, for that matter, halfway up an escalator. But, it's happened; you've committed yourselves to getting married and you've made it public by becoming engaged. Congratulations!

By the time you've made this decision you've already travelled quite a distance along the commitment road. No doubt you've talked a lot, shared many things about your past, opened up about your feelings, your interests, likes and dislikes. You've made yourselves vulnerable to each other and

24

declared your love. If you are Christians, you've prayed together with rather more closeness than you do with other believers. And you've probably cuddled quite a bit, too.

But now it's all growing in intensity. Quite properly you're becoming more intimate with one another. You are, after all, planning to spend the rest of your lives together. This raises few problems as far as talking about yourselves is concerned. In fact, you can hardly do too much of that. But what about the physical side of your relationship? How intimate should you let yourselves become in this area?

In cultures where marriages are arranged by the parents the issue scarcely arises because the couple concerned have very little contact with each other, and even that is heavily chaperoned. However, in the West we allow a very high degree of interaction between the sexes and a lot of freedom of choice in the conduct of our relationships. This means, in practice, that the majority of non-Christian couples indulge in sexual intercourse before they're married and certainly once they're engaged.

As we saw in the previous chapter, this runs counter to the will of God. Sexual intercourse is for marriage alone. Engagement is a commitment to enter that covenant; it isn't the covenant itself. So, from our Christian perspective it's wrong to have intercourse until you are actually married.

If you wish to have a God-honouring courtship you need to talk this through early on and agree that you'll save yourselves until your wedding day. This should also include agreeing not to bring one another to orgasm or climax by any form of mutual masturbation. The degree of intimacy which this involves belongs only within the marriage bond. Your purpose is to keep the spirit of God's word and not just the letter of the law.

Coming to this decision together will build security into your relationship and enhance your respect for each other's honour. Rather than creating a sense of frustration it will actually reduce the pressures and allow you to develop a more full-orbed knowledge of one another. Whether you are both still virgins or already sexually experienced we believe the will of God will prove to be 'good, pleasing and perfect' (Romans 12:2).

Nonetheless, sexual desires are very strong once you're engaged and it's important to know how to avoid going too far if you're to maintain your own standards. In the past, some have advised couples to play ultra-safe and to have virtually no physical contact at all. Feeling any desire for your loved one has been regarded as sinful. Somehow it's all meant to happen on the wedding night!

We'd like to reassure you straightaway that it's perfectly right and natural to have sexual feelings for each other. In fact, there would be something wrong with you if you didn't. You are in love, after all!

This is how God created us to be. It's part of the very stuff of love; what the Bible calls rather quaintly 'the way of a man with a maiden'. Instead of suppressing these feelings or being ashamed of them, you should thank the Lord for giving them to you. The last thing he wants is for you to have some kind of passionless, 'spiritual' romance. This earth desire to possess and to be possessed by the one you love has a heavenly origin.

So the real question boils down to this: how do we physically express these proper sexual desires in a manner which won't lead us to having intercourse before our wedding day?

To answer it and to help us understand how sexual arousal operates we're going to utilize a simple visual aid.

We want you to imagine your desires for one another as a river. Somewhere along its length is a waterfall. You can't actually see it yet, but you know it's not so very far away now that you're engaged. The current is persistent and grows stronger the nearer you get to the falls. It represents sexual arousal. There's a point where its power becomes irresistible and if you reach there you'll be swept over the falls; you won't be able to help having intercourse together. But all along the way there are pleasant bywaters where the current swirls and eddies but doesn't pull you towards the waterfall. These represent the demonstration of sexual affection.

The scene looks something like this:

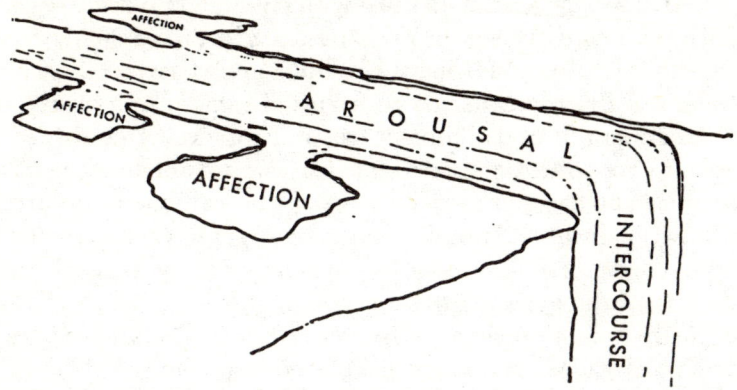

The secret of keeping your relationship within safe bounds lies in staying within the bywaters of sexual affection and avoiding the strong current of sexual arousal. Many get swept over the falls because either they underestimate the power of the current or they overestimate their own swimming skills. A few discover to their cost that they can't swim at all, while lots more spend their whole engagement desperately trying to hold out against the inevitable. Much better to enjoy splashing around in the pleasurable sidewaters without putting yourselves under this kind of pressure.

Your time together

We want to explain what this means in practical terms, and to begin with we'd suggest that the waterfall is always closer than most of us like to think. For this reason, as well as others, we don't think long engagements are a very good idea. Much depends upon your individual circumstances, of course, but generally speaking a year is quite adequate. Many of our friends have actually preferred engagements lasting no more than three to six months.

Setting the fulfilment of your promise to marry too far in the future can be the source of endless frustration—hardly a good start to life together. The apostle Paul wisely wrote, 'It is better to marry than to burn with passion' (1 Corinthians 7:9). If you are finding the pressures too great it may well be a sign that you should bring the wedding date forward. This is the sort of matter to discuss with trusted friends and advisors.

Keeping out of the current has much to do with how you spend your time together. If it consists mostly of being alone in a bedsit/bedroom or the back of the car, then you are asking for trouble. It makes much more sense to create your own chaperone situation by spending plenty of time in company and agreeing to short goodnights.

Rather than cutting yourselves off from others now that you're engaged, see more people. We've counselled more than one newly-wed couple who have returned from their honeymoon to wonder where all their friends have gone. The fact is they'd so isolated themselves over the months of their courtship that they'd lost contact with everyone. Make more friends together—go out with them, have meals, play games, do something useful. Incidentally, you'll learn an awful lot about each other in this way because some things only become clear as we see the person we love relating socially to others. Let your love be something shared with the whole community. Not least, it'll set you up as people who have an open home in the future, with lots of friends wanting to drop in on you.

Use your time to serve the Lord together in the life of your church. We don't know what your gifts and abilities are, but use them—practically, evangelistically, in children's work, home groups, or whatever. Spend time in prayer together. As you are now, so will you be when you are married.

Go for lots of long walks. Visit nice places. Make your time together romantic—candle-lit meals, flowers, enjoying God's creation together. We found walking and talking to be the most valuable part of our courtship and something which has carried on through the years of our marriage. We don't walk as much as we did but we haven't let up on the talking. It's far and away the best means of getting to know each other well. You can also talk out your moody times!

If you use your imagination you can create a very healthy and enjoyable environment for your engagement and you'll later look back on the time with many fond memories.

Affection and arousal

This brings us to the matter of how to handle the action. What we don't want to do is impose a set of rules on your behaviour. You'd only be tempted to break them anyway! Instead, we believe it's more helpful and responsible if you grasp the difference between the kind of physical contact which expresses sexual affection and that which is actually sexually arousing. This is partly concerned with *what* you do but also with the *spirit* in which you do it. For example, just stroking your fiancée's little finger can arouse her sexually, if that's what you're both wanting. But it's certainly acceptable to show your affection by caressing her hand. On the other hand (if you'll excuse the pun!), some physical contact will always be sexually arousing. We'll explain.

In general, sexual *affection* is something which can be expressed in public, quite openly, without embarrassing anybody or grieving the Holy Spirit. For example, holding hands, pecking on the cheek, a kiss on the lips, arms around each other's shoulders or waists, a short hug, lounging on the grass with your head on your partner's lap. These are the sort of pleasant gestures which demonstrate your love and care for one another. Actually, to see a couple behaving like that makes other people happy too. We recommend that you show plenty of this kind of affection. In fact, be very generous with it! It's the sort of thing we hope you'll carry on doing in public once you're married anyway.

The other kind of physical contact, which we believe you should avoid, is that which arouses you sexually. Once that begins to happen you'll find yourself caught in the current which leads to the waterfall. You'll either go over the top or be faced with a struggle to reach the safety of the bank.

As we've suggested, all sorts of caresses can be sexy depending upon the situation and your mood. Gentle prolonged stroking of the neck, ears, palms of the hands, backs of the arms, thighs and buttocks are all likely to have this effect. Prolonged mouth-to-mouth kissing, particularly when you entwine your tongues, is a sure-fire turn-on, as is protracted intense hugging too. It doesn't take long for a woman to discover the speed of male arousal when she suddenly finds this hard lump pressing against her groin. Be warned! You need to be fair to one another and allow yourselves very little of this kind of contact.

Incidentally, most young men get several erections a day. They pass off without any need for sexual relief. So it doesn't mean he's going to explode unless you have intercourse. Just cool the action and get back to the bywaters.

He no doubt thinks your breasts are very beautiful. And so he should. They aren't just there to feed babies. The Lover in the Song of Songs says to his Beloved:

> Your stature is like that of the palm, and your breasts like clusters of fruit. I said, 'I will climb the palm tree; I will take hold of its fruit' (Song of Songs 7:7–8).

But we believe you should wait until you're married before letting your man follow his example!

Caressing a woman's breasts is overtly arousing for a man and, in most cases, for the woman as well. That's even more true as far as your sexual organs are concerned. If you fondle one another there, whether under your clothes or on the outside, you'll find it very difficult not to be swept over the waterfall. This kind of contact is the prelude to intercourse so it's something you should avoid unless you intend going the whole way.

It's perhaps worth mentioning at this point that men are often turned on by what they see. Hence the pleasures of nakedness should be reserved until you are married. But you should also dress with a certain amount of discretion for your fiancé's sake. We're not suggesting that you appear dowdy or frumpy—by all means look your best—but avoid projecting an overprovocative image through what you wear. That's a matter for your own good taste to determine. There are no hard and fast rules in women's fashions!

Sexually arousing conduct really is unfair on one another if you're committed to remaining pure until you're married. It's a bit like having your favourite fattening food wafted under your nose when you're on a diet. Hardly helpful! Not only do you create needless tension and guilt but the repeated frustration of your desires can actually hinder your sexual adjustment after your wedding. If you are going to wait, it makes sense to do so in the bywaters of sexually affectionate behaviour.

As time progresses you'll doubtless need to reaffirm your commitment not to have intercourse together. There will inevitably be times when your hands will stray beyond affection into arousal. You must be honest about this and agree to return to your previous limits. Even though you've moved downstream you can still find another safe sidewater.

By the time you reach the week preceding your wedding day you may find that in spite of all your efforts you've drifted to a bywater well within sight and sound of the waterfall. Provided you've sought to act responsibly, there's no need to feel that you've failed each other because of this. But at the same time, because you are so near, it's even more essential that you continue to act with restraint when you're together. Having kept yourselves thus far, there's no point in throwing it all away when the goal is in sight. So, although it's good to see each other during this busy time—otherwise you can feel a bit like strangers at the wedding—we believe you should lean deliberately on the side of caution as far as your physical contact is concerned. In just a few days you'll be free to enjoy one another to the full for the rest of your lives. You can afford to wait until then.

*   *   *

This is our counsel for a God-honouring courtship, and one which we believe is also realistic. Right paths are seldom the easiest to follow. It's far simpler to behave like everyone else—ignore God's laws, go on the pill, and have intercourse as you please. So let's ask the question once more: is it really worth waiting?

God doesn't command pre-marital purity because he's a kill-joy. He does it for our good because he knows how we're made. We're in his image, not just animals with instincts. Sexual intercourse has a mystery about it, what the Bible calls 'knowing' your partner. You become 'one flesh' and it changes you for ever. The depth of that experience requires no less than a total life commitment, a covenant, to make it truly fulfilling.

You have something very precious to anticipate. Your honeymoon will be special, instead of an anticlimax because you've done it all already. Yours will be the beautiful unveiling of the mystery of love. That's worth waiting for.

One of the problems we've commonly encountered with folk who've had intercourse before they were married is that the thrill went out of it once they were wed. Sexual adjustment is then quite difficult to come by. The reason is this: if you initiate your sexual experience upon the thrill of secrecy, of danger and of being 'naughty', once that's taken away by marriage there's very little stimulus left. You then have to undo the damage before you can start again. Following God's way, however, means your sexual awakening will be to the thrill of pure love—and that lasts a lifetime!

Want any more convincing? No fear of pregnancy. Christians are at a higher risk when they indulge in pre-marital sex because they tend not to use birth control. After all, that would be pre-meditated sin, wouldn't it? No stress and strain of having to say no. No angry recriminations, let alone regrets and resentments if you do go too far.

You'll have treated one another with respect. Self-control and strength of character will have been built into your lives—a fruit of the Spirit that will stand you in good stead later on.

Above all else, you'll have the joy of knowing you obeyed the Lord. No guilt and no regrets. Just his blessing. Surely that's the best way. Why settle for less?

3

Body Facts

Human sexual love is one of the most fascinating of all God's works. The attraction between a boy and girl, the marvellous manner in which a husband and wife fit so pleasurably together, the way babies are produced; it is perhaps the crowning masterpiece of all creation.

But, fascinating as it is, you don't need to understand it all, either to make love or to have babies. After all, you don't have to know all about your digestive system in order to enjoy food, or to go to the loo! It's much more important to know where the taps are and how to turn them on than to have a complete grasp of the whole plumbing system.

The aim of this chapter is to tell you what you've got, how it works and how intercourse takes place, but without getting you bogged down with too much technical detail. We're going to do this with the aid of some diagrams, and the help of a chirpy little guide.

'Hallo, my name is Fred Zoon and I'm a sperm. Actually, I'm a spermatozoon, but only people in white coats call me that. I'm a rather friendly creature, you'll find. There's about five hundred million of us in this batch and we've just landed at the neck of Jane's womb. She's married to Tim, by the way, and they've just had intercourse. But I'd better tell you where it all started, hadn't I?

34

'I began life about three days ago in Tim's body. Well, a bit outside of it really because I was made in one of his testicles—his friends call them balls. He's got two of these, though he could manage just as well with one. They hang between his legs, one slightly lower than the other, in a crinkly sac called the scrotum.

'These testicles are like giant beans, about 4cm long and two across and they make sperms like me all day long. Millions of us. We all look like microscopic tadpoles with small heads and long tails. We're all natural born swimmers—that's what our tails are for—and our heads may be small but we're jam-packed with info. In fact, I've got enough in mine to half change the world—if only I can find the other half. She's an egg-head called Ova, by the way, somewhere in Jane.

'Tim's testicles also make a hormone called testosterone which goes straight into his bloodstream and helps him look like a man—muscles, deep voice, hairy and all that. You'd better tell Jane not to squeeze them or knock them 'cos they're rather tender and Tim won't half let her know it if she does!

'Anyway, as fast as we're made we get shoved along into this unpronounceable hairlike tube all coiled up on the top side of each testicle. That's where we mature. Then just as we're getting comfy we're pushed up into Tim's body along a tube called the vas deferens till we reach our next staging post called the ampulla. I tell you, it's all go. Sheer weight of numbers, I reckon.

'Well, Tim and Jane decided to have intercourse. Very interesting that. But I'd better start with what they do it with, hadn't I?

'Tim's got this thing called a penis, though it gets called an awful lot of other things as well, but we'll leave it at that. Normally it's soft and anything from about 5–10cm long. Varies with the weather, I always say. Amazing bit of engineering, it is. Mostly it's three columns of what they call erectile tissue. When Tim gets sexually aroused blood pours into this tissue and his penis grows long and hard. That's called an erection and it means he's ready for intercourse. Actually, Tim gets erections at all sorts of odd times, quite often before he's been to the loo first thing in the morning. He's not sex mad or anything; it's just the way it is—very subliminal!

'Take a look at this diagram so you can get an idea of how God designed it.

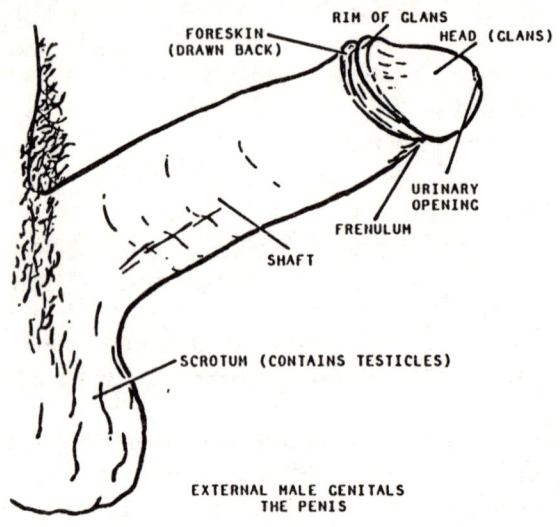

EXTERNAL MALE GENITALS
THE PENIS

'Erect penes (plural, that is) vary in length like everything else. They tell me the average is about 13–18 cm long, but it doesn't much matter. You can't change it anyway, and it's no sign of virility. The secret of successful loving is in a man's brain, not his groin. So tell Tim not to get fussed about it.

'That top bit, the head or glans, is very sensitive and designed to give them both pleasure. The rim is harder than the tip and rubs on Jane's insides. But the most sensitive part is just underneath the head—it's a small connecting membrane called the frenulum.

'Some men have got foreskins, others haven't. If they haven't it's because it's been cut off. That's called circumcision. It doesn't affect sexual performance one way or the other but it's important for Tim to wash this bit every day, especially if he's still got a foreskin. See, the glands under there produce a stuff called smegma which can go off.

'Anyway, that's enough about him for the moment. Let me tell you what Jane's got. This is how the good Lord made her from the outside and the whole thing's called the vulva.

'Those outer lips are two thick folds of flesh covered with hair and that's just about all you can see when she's not sexually aroused.

'The inner lips are two thinner folds of skin which are

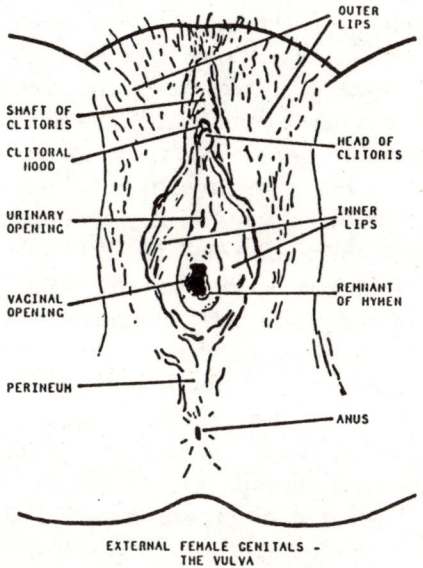

EXTERNAL FEMALE GENITALS –
THE VULVA

crinkled on the outside and smooth and moist on the inside. Jane might as well know that they vary in size, shape and colour from woman to woman. Some are almost totally covered by the outer lips, others hang out a bit. It doesn't matter. In any case, when Jane is aroused they thicken and part easily.

'Where these inner lips meet at the front is Jane's most

important organ for sexual pleasure. It's called the clitoris and the only reason it's there is for Jane's sexual enjoyment—so I guess God wants women to have fun too! As a matter of fact, they're the only female species in all creation who can experience orgasm.

'Anyhow, the clitoris is similar to Tim's penis, only much smaller. It's actually about 1½–3cm long, with a small moulded tip called the glans which is partly covered with a fold of skin. Unlike Tim's penis, Jane's clitoris is mostly hidden but it may grow a bit when she's sexually excited. Some do, some don't. Either way she'll still enjoy it if Tim does his stuff properly.

'Below the clitoris is the hole where urine comes out and then beneath that is the entrance to Jane's vagina. When she was a virgin this was partly covered with a membrane called the hymen. It was never completely blocked and if she used internal tampons for her periods the hymen would've been stretched quite a bit. Sometimes it gets broken if a girl is active in sport, but usually it's the first act of intercourse that does it. Because there are small blood vessels in it a little harmless bleeding may occur when this takes place. If that first penetration is done properly it won't be terribly painful.

'Well, as I say, they decided to have intercourse and aroused each other. Tim's penis grew erect and various glands in and around Jane's vagina began to produce a lubricant so that she became moist and slippery down there. That's so everything will slide in and out easily and feel nice.

'Then Tim pushed his erect penis into her vagina. This is a tube of pink, wrinkled skin only about 8–12cm long and normally held closed by muscles near the entrance. But Jane doesn't have to worry about being big enough to accommodate Tim, 'cos God has designed the whole thing on a flexi-fit system. Her vagina can stretch enough to allow a baby's head through—and Tim's not that big, I can tell you! What happens when they have intercourse is that it naturally shapes itself around his penis.

'Well now, there we all were, waiting in the old ampulla

when things began to stir. Very clever is this next bit, but you'd best have a quick look at another diagram to make sense of it.

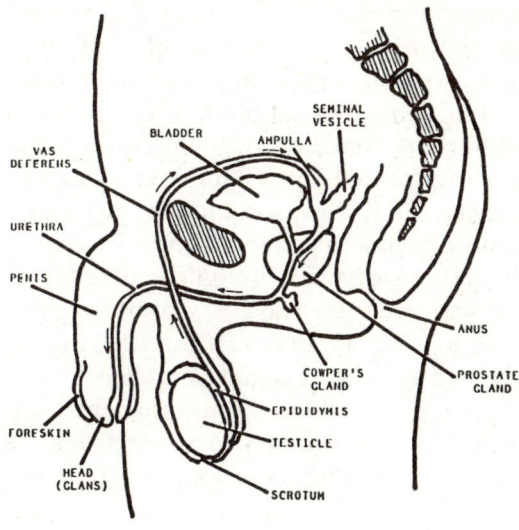

MAN'S REPRODUCTIVE SYSTEM

'There's this valve that shuts off Tim's bladder when he's having intercourse so he can't go to the loo at the same time. That's a relief, eh, Jane? Then there's this Cowper's gland which oozes some neutralizing fluid into the urethra—a sort of disinfectant to keep the likes of me safe.

'I said I'm a good swimmer, didn't I? Well, those seminal vesicles give me something to swim in. The prostate gland does the same. That gland is spring loaded as well; it's part of the firing mechanism which launches me on the journey of my life.

'Anyhow, Tim was sliding his penis rhythmically in and out of Jane's vagina and she was matching his thrusts by rocking her pelvis. Kind of comes naturally. Then they began to get faster and faster. All of a sudden Jane's body went rigid, she clung to Tim as this intense sexual feeling spread out from her clitoris and flooded her body while a series of muscular spasms rippled through her womb. That and a tremendous emotional release is what makes up her orgasm, or climax as they sometimes call it.

'It was much the same for Tim, only the muscular spasms came from the base of his penis. It also affected us 'cos a moment later we were on the move, and do I mean move! We were mixed up with seminal fluid, forced past the prostate gland and fairly rocketed down the urethra. A fraction of a second later we spurted out of Tim's penis in several squirts of white, sticky fluid. If it wasn't for the fact that we hit the neck of Jane's womb we could've gone anything from 30–60cm. Altogether we were swimming in about 5–10cc of this stuff called semen. By the way, we're quite hygienic, so Jane doesn't need to wash us out or anything like that afterwards.

'Once he had ejaculated, Tim's penis began to shrink back to its former size and he withdrew from his satisfied wife leaving us lot here. Now this is what Jane's insides look like just so as you'll know where I'm speaking from.

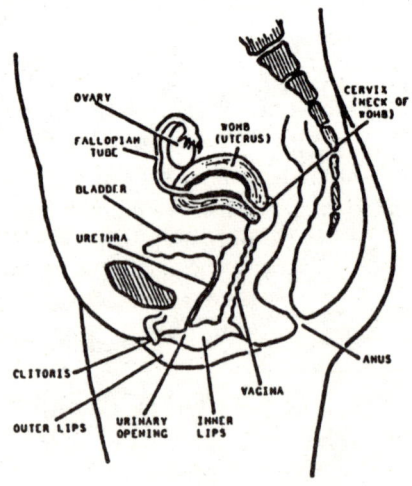

WOMAN'S REPRODUCTIVE SYSTEM

'What happens to me next? Well, I've got to start swimming, haven't I? Programmed that way. See those ovaries up there? They make eggs called ova and push them into the fallopian tubes. If I get there and there's one waiting I might get to fertilize it. But I've got a lot of competition—about 500 million to be precise. So here goes, must Zoon off—get it? Oi, stop shoving, lads! Into the great unknown...but that's another story.

Your ever-loving sperm,
Fred Zoon.'

We hope you enjoyed reading about yourselves like that and that you'll appreciate even more the Lord's incredible designs. The psalmist says, 'I praise you because I am fearfully and wonderfully made; your works are wonderful, I know that full well' (Psalm 139:14).

Of course, some folk do think they're more fearfully than wonderfully made and we just want to say a word about that in case it applies to you.

Our pal, Fred, has already implied that your penis is the right size. You may be shorter or longer than the average, but provided you know what to do with it you'll satisfy your bride. As for your ability to maintain an erection or to reach orgasm, don't worry about it. Anxiety itself is the great deflator! You're going to be all right on the night if you just take things naturally. And if you're a virgin, lack of previous experience doesn't mean lack of ability.

We live in a world where every woman is supposed to look like a cover girl, so unless you do, there's a special temptation for you to feel physically inadequate. How many girls do you know who are happy with the size and shape of their breasts, for example? Let alone noses, teeth, hair, legs....

Then what about your sexual organs themselves? You may only have identified that bit of your body with the basic functions of life. Indeed, your periods and daily secretions may have made you think of that part as messy.

That's all going to change as you get married. Your breasts

will be your husband's delight and your vulva a thing of beauty and pleasure to him. Listen to the Song of Songs again: 'How beautiful you are and how pleasing, O love, with your delights! Your stature is like that of the palm, and your breasts like clusters of fruit' (Song of Songs 7:6–7). The same book describes the girl's sexual organs in the symbolism of a garden, and chapter 7, verse 2 can be properly translated, 'Your vulva is a rounded goblet that never lacks blended wine.'

So God wants you not to be ashamed of those parts. They're an aspect of your total beauty. You may not think you're the right shape or even that you've got all the bits. Don't worry. You're the shape that will please your husband and you'll soon find out that it's all there. Accept yourself as God made you—just right for your man to love and appreciate.

One last word. We've used standard medical names to describe the bits and bobs. But you don't want your bedroom to sound like a biology lesson. One of the joys of married life is creating your own private sexual communication system. Invent some pet names of your own for the intimate parts. Try to be a bit more imaginative than 'thing' or, 'Do you want "it" tonight?' The Song of Songs uses a number of words with double meaning, so you can, too. That way you'll not only avoid both the world's crudities and its clinical terms, but you'll have something special that belongs to you two alone.

4

Birth Control

At some point during your engagement you'll need to talk about contraception and how many children you want. Leave it too late and you'll be shutting the stable door after the horse has bolted, so to speak!

Non-Christian couples have just one question to face: what form of contraception to use. Loyal Roman Catholics have even that answered for them—the Vatican only approves of the rhythm method. But as Bible-believing Christians you need to begin with the question: is it right to use birth control at all?

Now you may already have decided in your own minds that for purely practical reasons and because nearly everyone else does, you are going to use some kind of contraception. But we think it's a good thing to at least consider the fors and againsts, if only to make certain you've come to your decision on spiritual grounds and not just followed the crowd.

So, to get your discussion under way, here are the usual main points given on each side.

The case against using birth control

1. The command 'be fruitful and multiply' has never been cancelled and so intercourse should always include the intent of having children.

43

2. God is the giver of all life. He's the One who opens and closes the womb. We shouldn't play God by seeking to take into our hands what belongs to him.

3. Christians who use contraceptives do so because they're motivated by secular expectations concerning their lifestyle rather than by the will of God.

Arguments in favour of using birth control

1. The command 'be fruitful and multiply' was given only at those times in history when it was needed. There comes a point, both for mankind in general and for every child-bearing couple in particular, when they have fulfilled the command. Knowing when a family is complete is a matter to be decided prayerfully before God.

2. You don't have intercourse just to conceive babies. Its primary purpose is to express 'one flesh'. Children should be the fruit of that union at some time, but not all the time. A woman's periodic cycle makes it possible to conceive for only a few days a month, but the Bible doesn't forbid intercourse on all but those days. On the contrary, Paul says, 'Do not deprive each other except by mutual consent and for a time, so that you may devote yourselves to prayer' (1 Corinthians 7:5).

3. God gives life very generously, i.e. most wombs are 'open'. He only occasionally 'closes' the womb, and then it warrants specific mention in the Scriptures.

4. God uses human means to reproduce life. We're involved and that means we have to work in responsible co-operation with him. If we sow, we will reap. If we don't, we won't. The same principle applies to human reproduction as to spiritual. Paul wrote, 'I planted the seed, Apollos watered it, but God made it grow' (1 Corinthians 3:6).

We appreciate that none of the arguments on either side are conclusive—that's why we've given them for you to think about. Our own opinion is that it's appropriate to use some form of birth control if you don't want children. You may, of course, disagree with us. We don't mind. But if you do choose not to employ contraceptives you will, in all likelihood, soon be expecting your first baby. You must be really peaceful with this prospect and receive the pregnancy gladly as a gift of God. It's no use saying, 'We're leaving it to the Lord,' and then complaining!

We should add that we believe love-making is intended to produce fruit at some time. Speaking of marital faithfulness, the prophet Malachi writes, 'Has not the Lord made them one? In flesh and spirit they are his. And why one? Because he was seeking godly offspring' (Malachi 2:15). It's been our personal joy to make love together for over twenty years and to raise three super children who love the Lord. Love without children is like an apple tree without apples. We hope you'll want some of your own.

Incidentally, the time to have children is not when you can afford it, or when you've done all the things you ever wanted to do together, but when you sense it's God's time. It may be sooner or later on, but if you live by faith you will know. Don't be guided by secular expectations.

If you do decide to use birth control, then you'll have to make up your minds as to what kind. This ought to be a joint decision; you mustn't leave it to one or the other of you. After all, it affects both your lives.

There are a variety of options available with varying degrees of reliability, safety and comfort in use. We've listed them in alphabetical order together with the information which we think you'll find helpful.

Abortion

It may not have occurred to you to consider abortion as a form of birth control, but as a way of preventing the birth of an unwanted baby it's reckoned to be the most commonly used method in the world, accounting for the termination of one in four known pregnancies.

Under English law abortion is not an offence provided certain criteria are met. While some of these are intended to be genuinely merciful provisions to save the endangered life of a mother, or to deal with the rare cases of pregnancy arising from rape or incest, the vast majority of abortions are performed under the dubious grounds of risk to the mental or physical health of the mother or existing children. The fact that every pregnancy entails some risk means, in effect, that any woman can use the law to obtain an abortion. This puts us effectively in the same position as the United States where the law is positively framed to make abortion a legal right. A woman may simply say she doesn't want the baby and request an abortion.

Without wishing to discuss the whole issue in this book, we wish to state unequivocally that we believe abortion used in this way as a form of birth control is wrong. It is the wilful taking of a human life, a form of murder. We are not simply dealing with 'foetal matter' but with a God-given person. 'For you created my inmost being; you knit me together in my mother's womb...your eyes saw my unformed body' (Psalm 139:13, 16).

We have to make a stand and call society to repent of its sacrifice of children to its materialistic gods. Women need to be warned that this 'easy' option demands a price not only in possible long-term physical and emotional damage but in certain blood-guiltiness before God. This method isn't for Christians; we've only included it in order to make what we believe to be a necessary point, particularly as increasing numbers of pregnant women are confronted with the option when they report to their doctor.

Cap and spermicide

Because of reactions against using the pill (see below), the barrier cap is growing in popularity again. It's very safe to use, except for rare cases of allergy to the spermicide.

There are various designs, but the diaphragm is the most

common. This consists of a thin rubber dome mounted on a flexible metal rim. It's inserted into the vagina by the woman prior to intercourse so that it fits over the cervix (the neck of the womb), where it acts as a barrier to the sperm getting any further. Practical reliability is about 83% but it can be as high as 98% if used consistently and with a spermicide. This is a sperm-killing gel, cream or aerosol spray which is smeared on the cap, especially the rim, just before it's inserted. More spermicide, often in pessary form, is then introduced into the vagina.

You can obtain a cap from your Family Planning Clinic. They will find one the right size for you. This is important. The fit has to be checked every six months and also if your weight changes by more than 3kg, or you miscarry or have a baby. The clinic will give you full instructions on how to use it. In practice it is no more difficult than inserting a sanitary tampon. You must leave it in place for at least six hours after intercourse and insert more spermicide if you don't have intercourse within two hours of putting it in. When you do remove the cap, simply rinse it under warm water, pat dry and replace in its plastic case. Check every so often for punctures.

If you've put the cap in properly, neither of you will detect its presence during intercourse. The only real problem is that you do have to pre-meditate making love. Which is fine most of the time, but if you suddenly decide to leap on one another in the kitchen one Saturday afternoon, you'd better have a condom handy, or take the risk!

A recent development of the cap is a mushroom-shaped job which is impregnated with a powerful spermicide and lasts up to twenty-four hours, however many times you have intercourse. It's called the sponge and has the advantage of being unmessy. At the moment reliability is only 73–85%. It's also quite expensive—you use it for one day and then throw it away—and it could cause complications if you forget to remove it.

Condom

Variously known as the sheath, french letter, rubber, or Durex (after the trade name), the condom is a popular, 90%-effective contraceptive, free of side effects. It consists of a thin rubber tube sealed at one end and which is rolled over the erect penis so that when a man ejaculates the semen is trapped in the end. Used consistently, especially with a spermicide, its reliability can be virtually 100%.

Condoms are readily available on chemist's counters, in men's hairdressers, at Family Planning Clinics or by mail order. They are all a standard 18cm long and come in a variety of colours, textures and lubrications. The only thing that really matters is to buy a reliable brand. It's best to obtain the teat-ended type as these are less likely to burst.

To use a condom, remove it carefully from its foil sachet and unroll it about 2cm, then place it over your erect penis and roll the rest down the length of the shaft. Either of you can do this as part of your love-making just before you actually engage in intercourse. You shouldn't use any other lubricant on your penis or the sheath will slip off. And be careful not to puncture it with your fingernails.

After you've climaxed and before your erection goes down you must withdraw your penis from your wife, holding the condom so that it doesn't come off until you are well clear of her. It can then be removed and thrown away later.

The only real problem with the sheath seems to be the users' temperaments. Some couples feel putting it on interrupts their love play, others complain that it's like making love separated by a plastic bag, and some men claim it reduces sensitivity too much. You must find out for yourselves.

Intra-Uterine Device

IUDs, objects inserted in the womb to prevent pregnancy, have been around for a long time. Today they are generally made of polyethylene plastic and come in a variety of shapes. Some are plain while others are wound with copper wire. The plain ones can be left in the womb for many years, whereas the copper-wound ones need exchanging every two or three years. Generally speaking, IUDs are not recommended for women who have never been pregnant because of the risk of infection or other complications.

IUDs are introduced into the womb via the vagina by a doctor, either in the surgery or at a suitable out-patient's clinic. The process may produce some vaginal bleeding and a bit of pain for a couple of days. Once inserted, however, the device is undetectable except for two nylon threads which are left protruding from the cervix so that the woman can check it's still there (expulsion of the IUD during the first year is not uncommon).

The IUD is about 95% effective and is easily removed if pregnancy is desired, but it does present some problems. Women fitted with them often complain of heavy periods and pain. Up to 20% have the device removed as a result. There is also an increased risk of pelvic inflammatory disease. However, a new, hormone-releasing IUD appears actually to reduce menstrual bleeding and to *protect* against pelvic infection.

Many Christians have problems with the way an IUD functions. Although it is not absolutely clear, the consensus of medical opinion is that it either prevents the implantation of a fertilized ovum in the womb or dislodges it from the uterus lining. If you believe that a fertilized ovum is a human baby, then the moral considerations which apply to abortion are relevant here also.

Pill

Once hailed as the solution to all our problems the contraceptive pill is easy to use, readily available, offers total freedom in love-making and, if taken correctly, is almost 100% effective. It also regulates periods and for many women reduces pre-menstrual tension and period pains. However, in recent years concerns have been voiced both about discomforts and the health risks which accompany its use.

Many women complain of nausea, sore breasts, tiredness, weight increase, swollen ankles, and headaches, especially for the first two or three months. Others get moody and depressed. Some claim reduced sex drive, vaginal dryness and bad discharges. Wearers of contact lenses may suffer sore eyes.

More serious are the long-term dangers of thrombosis, hypertension, heart disease and breast cancer. Women already suffering from epilepsy, diabetes, high blood pressure or heart trouble are particularly at risk and, notably, all women who smoke. These problems increase with age.

Before you get scared off we should point out that the risk of serious illness, i.e. thrombosis or cancer, is very small, particularly for non-smoking women under thirty-five, who are otherwise healthy. And many women find the discomforts minimal after only a short while.

There are many different brands of contraceptive pill available but they all fall into two categories: the Combined Pill containing the two hormones, oestrogen and progesterone, and the Progesterone Only Pill (POP), also known as the mini-pill. All combined pills for normal use contain much smaller hormone doses than their predecessors. For this reason they are sometimes called mini-pills as well.

To avoid this confusion you should ask for either the Combined Pill or the Progesterone Only Pill when you go to your GP or Family Planning Clinic. Both are highly reliable but they work in somewhat different ways. In view of the health risks, you should insist on a combined pill with the lowest dosage of both hormones or, better still, the POP. The only thing to remember about the latter is that you must take it without fail at the same time every day for maximum effectiveness. If you find that difficult you'll be better off with a combined pill.

If you choose this form of contraception you should start

taking the pill about two months before your wedding day. Your doctor can advise you on the timing so that you can at least guarantee not having a period on your honeymoon. Incidentally, a gynaecological examination is quite unnecessary if you are a young virgin in good health, but it is advised if you are older or already sexually experienced.

All in all you should encounter few difficulties if you adhere to these guidelines: a) obtain the POP version if possible; b) stop using it and go over to another kind of contraceptive three months before you want to have a baby; c) don't use it if you are over thirty years of age or if you are much overweight, of slow metabolism or have any serious health complaint; d) if you get the minor side effects and they don't clear up in two to three months, either change to another brand or try a different contraceptive method; e) receive regular health checks from your GP or Family Planning Clinic.

Rhythm

Otherwise known as 'Vatican roulette' (because it's the only method allowed to Roman Catholics and about as safe as Russian roulette!) or 'rhythm and blues' (because if you use no other method you'll have to abstain for at least ten days a month). Maybe you've heard the joke: 'What do they call a man and woman who use the rhythm method?' Answer: Mummy and Daddy!

But, jesting apart, for those people who prefer the minimum 'interference with nature' it's a viable option.

You probably already know that women are not fertile all the time but only when they ovulate, that is, when an egg becomes available for fertilization, which happens once a month. So if you avoid intercourse around that time, which is about fourteen days before your next period, you'll be safe. This is the basic idea behind the rhythm method. What makes the unsafe period longer is the fact that sperm can live for three to four days in your womb and ovulation can occur any time from the thirteenth to the seventeenth day. Here's a diagram to explain 'safe' and 'unsafe' days, taking the first day of your period as day one.

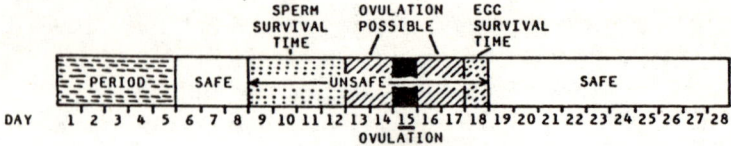

RHYTHM METHOD CALCULATION

This method, using the calendar, assumes you are one of the only 8% of women who have a regular twenty-eight-day cycle. If you don't, then you'll need to keep twelve months' record of the length of your cycles (i.e. from the beginning of one period to the beginning of the next). What you then do is subtract eighteen from the number of days of your shortest cycle to find your first unsafe day. You find the last unsafe day by subtracting ten from the length of your longest cycle. Example: shortest cycle twenty-four days, subtract eighteen is six; longest cycle thirty-two days, subtract ten is twenty-two. So, *unsafe* time is from the sixth to the twenty-second day, counting from the first day of your period. Get a friend to help you if you don't like maths!

Another way of finding out when you're safe *after* ovulation is to take your temperature daily with a rectal or Basal Body Temperature thermometer. You do this every day before getting out of bed in the morning. By this means you note your normal body temperature. When it rises by 0.6°C (1°F) you have ovulated. Your temperature stays up until the beginning of your next period. You are safe from three days after you note the rise. This does not tell you when you cease to be safe before ovulation and, of course, colds and flu do mess it up a bit.

One other rhythm observation you can make is to examine the state of the mucus around your cervix. This natural excretion increases in volume and becomes thinner, more slippery and clear around the time of ovulation. The safe time before ovulation is when there's a moderate amount of thick and cloudy mucus. When it begins to thin and becomes a mixture of cloudy and clear you are unsafe. Later on when there's only a tiny amount, which is also thick and cloudy, you are safe again. This test can be done by inserting your finger into your vagina. Needless to say, you have to gain some experience in making this kind of observation and it must be combined with the calendar and temperature method to be anything like accurate.

The rhythm method is completely natural but only 75–80% reliable.

If you use this form of contraception you would be well advised to adopt the condom or the cap during your unsafe time, or use some form of sexual release other than intercourse. Taking into account your period as well, you may only be able to have intercourse for fifteen days a month at most relying on rhythm alone—that's quite a lot of abstinence for a couple in their sexual prime!

Sterilization

For a young couple this is not really an option to consider because, at the present, sterilization operations are more or less irreversible. However, once you have your family and are sure you're not to have more children, it's an excellent form of contraception which sets you totally free in love-making, carries no long-term health risks and is virtually 100% effective.

Being irreversible, you have to make a careful joint decision facing questions such as, 'What if all our children are killed in a car crash?' 'Supposing baby Simon dies of something?' 'What if one of us died and the remaining partner remarried and wanted more children?' Generally speaking you shouldn't contemplate sterilization before thirty to thirty-five years of age.

Either one of you can be sterilized. For a man the operation is called a vasectomy and can be performed in a small clinic or even by your GP under a local anaesthetic. It consists of making two small incisions in the scrotum and severing each vas deferens. The ends are tied off and the incisions stitched. It only takes a few minutes.

The operation will leave you shuffling bow-legged for two or three days with that feeling of what is euphemistically called 'a groin injury' by sports commentators. Don't plan to drive from the clinic yourself! But you'll soon recover.

The operation prevents sperm from getting along the tubes. Instead, they are simply reabsorbed by your body. You don't lose your virility or your ability to ejaculate (semen is still emitted, but without sperm) and there are no after-effects. Because some sperm may be lurking in the plumbing, it's wise to use some other contraceptive for three to four months until a check confirms the semen free from sperm.

Sterilizing a woman consists of cutting or blocking the Fallopian tubes, which carry eggs from the ovaries to the womb, so that the ova are harmlessly reabsorbed by the body. Nowadays, this is most commonly performed by making a tiny incision near the navel and inserting an instrument which both allows the surgeon to see inside the abdomen and to cauterize the tubes, so sealing them. This is done under general anaesthetic but needs only one or two days in hospital. The scar will virtually vanish in a few months.

A recent development is the use of silicone plugs or a glue which causes tissue to grow in the tubes. This is 'gunned' into the tubes via the vagina and involves no surgery.

Withdrawal

An unreliable method in which the man withdraws his penis at the crucial moment and ejaculates outside his wife's body and well away from her vulva. Its unreliability is due to the fact that some sperm 'leak out' before ejaculation in that fluid which cleanses the urethra.

Psychologically it is very unsatisfactory for both partners. There is a real danger of turning your climax into an anti-climax. We don't recommend it.

New developments are always taking place. For example, just becoming available is a small implant in the arm which daily releases a tiny dose of the hormone, levonorgestrel, for up to five years. It can be removed at any time and is very effective. Because the dose is much smaller than even the POP it should be safer.

Research continues into reversible sterilization techniques, once-a-month pills—and the elusive male pill.

All this lot may make you wonder whether it's worth it! Whatever happened to story book love-making in all its romantic simplicity? Well, this is the way it is in real life. There is no 'perfect' contraceptive. You have to find out what you have most peace in using. For what it's worth, our recommendation to you as a newly-wed couple would be either the Progesterone Only Pill or a combination of rhythm and cap or rhythm and sheath. Once you have your family, sterilization is a good long-term option. But you must make up your own minds. Don't be afraid to take advice from married friends as well—they at least have some experience.

And if, when all's said and done, you get pregnant, remember your life is in God's hands and so is the baby's. Don't panic, but trust him and love your child. It's amazing how many 'accidents' prove to be the will of God.

THE HONEYMOON

We've written this section particularly with the needs of 'first-timers' in mind, though it contains advice which will help all who are anticipating their honeymoon. The three chapters cover preparations for the wedding night, how to make love together for the first time, and what to do about any minor problems which may occur.

5

Have You Packed Everything?

What a palaver it is getting married!

'Have you given the certificate to the pastor?'

'Are you sure the banns were read?'

'I don't even know what "plighting my troth" means.'

'You're not serious about inviting Auntie Flo, are you?'

'Do you have to have all these church people to the reception?'

'Going to cost me a fortune as it is.'

'Now, have you ordered the flowers, cars, photographer, suit...?'

'You'll never be ready in time at this rate.'

'Well, it's a girl's privilege to be late.'

'I don't know why you're marrying him in the first place.'

Be warned, it's an exhausting time and you'll be mightily relieved just to get down the aisle in one piece with most people there and looking more or less as they should. But for all that, it'll be a very happy occasion and when you've made your vows before God and everyone else you'll know it's all been worth it. You're married—at last!

But it's not over yet. There's the photographs and reception, the speeches, saying hello to all the unknown relatives, having the car vandalized by your friends.... Not until then will you get away on your honeymoon.

That, of course, is the other big event to anticipate; your

first night together. But are honeymoons all they're cracked up to be? Is it worth spending all that money to make love in a strange hotel room rather than in your own new home? Let alone self-consciously trying not to look like newly-weds when you so obviously are!

It's a matter of personal opinion, of course, and we don't know how well off you are financially, but we do strongly suggest that you plan to get away for a honeymoon—if only because you'll both be ready for a break by then. Even a few days will help refresh you, and the time away together without distractions, when you can give each other your undivided attention, is an excellent way of starting out on your new life. And your first physical union as husband and wife is worthy of a special setting, after all.

However, it's no use expecting to have a first night full of romance, passion and wonderful discovery if you're both so dead beat that you can hardly keep your eyes open. So, you'll need to conserve some energy for the occasion—and that's to do with planning.

It's advisable not to fix the time of your wedding too late in the day. We've shared in countless marriages and have come to the conclusion that midday or thereabouts is by far the best time for the ceremony. That gives ample opportunity for all the far-flung relatives to arrive, and for you to get yourselves ready. It means that everyone will be eating by around 2 pm. And it will allow you two to get away at a reasonable hour when it's all over.

Unless you're exceptionally energetic types we recommend you don't stay on to an evening party. By all means let everybody else have one—but you have something better to do!

Where you go, home or abroad, near or far, is up to you and your pocket but we do advise you not to make too long a journey on your actual wedding day. If you're intending to stay in this country, find a relatively local hotel or guesthouse for an overnight stop and then continue further afield the next day. Otherwise plan for a main destination not more than 50–100 miles' drive away.

If you're travelling abroad then either arrange to reach your resort at a reasonable hour or again find a hotel in this country for the night and make the flight not too early the next day. You can, of course, have the night in your own home—but beware of those 'friends' who did your car!

Whatever your arrangements, by planning it this way you'll avoid arriving at your honeymoon suite late at night absolutely shattered and fit for nothing.

Privacy is important, especially for first-timers, so do try to find a secluded place together. We've known of more than one couple who have spent their honeymoon with a church houseparty and had to suffer endless ribald comments about shaking walls, bouncing ceilings and squeaky bedsprings from their companions! Let alone the embarrassment of walking into breakfast late every morning. You'll be better off without that.

Very probably, you'll buy quite a few new clothes for going away in. We'd just like to say a word about your underwear and night things. Or, to put it another way, a precious gift is worth wrapping up in something nice.

From the moment you're married life changes. You enter a realm of sexual intimacy and freedom. But you also take on the responsibility of bringing pleasure to your other half, and that includes deliberately setting out to be attractive to one another. No longer do you dress indifferently or to please yourself, but to delight your partner. This is especially the case with those garments which herald the naked joy of Christian love-making.

Now your wife is very unlikely to be *seduced* by your underwear or pyjamas. That's just not how it works. But every woman appreciates a bit of style in her man. Old fashioned underwear looks comic, so go for something with a bit of dash. Have a change from those pale blue Y-fronts you've been buying for years. Get something with a bit of colour and cut. If you wear pyjamas—and you don't have to, of course—take a look at yourself in the mirror and ask if they're what you'd want to see in the morning if you were her.

Men are completely different from women in this respect. Unlike women, they are very much turned on by what they see. How you look matters a lot to your husband. So what, in particular, can you do about your lingerie?

Many girls choose underclothes which keep their mothers happy or raise no eyebrows with the other girls in the flat. Or they go for warmth and durability. But that's hardly the stuff for romantic nights. Buy something lighter, briefer, more transparent than you've worn before, or go for some silky, slinky garments—whatever will show you off to your seductive best. Pack an alluring nightie; be a bit extravagant. Ask him what his favourite colours are.

Remember, from now on your aim is to delight one another. Don't allow yourself to be influenced by this 'you're just being treated as a sex object' stuff. What nonsense! You light his fire and you can be sure you'll never go cold yourself. Your honeymoon is a good place to start looking unashamedly sexy for this man who has promised to give his whole life for you. Neither of you will ever regret pleasing each other.

Anything else? Don't forget to pack the contraceptives. You're not going to run out of sheaths or pills are you? Put your cap and spermicide with your washing things. Make sure, both of you, that you know how to use your contraceptives. You don't want to be all fingers and thumbs on the night or stuck in the loo for half an hour trying to get a diaphragm in place.

You can if you wish stretch your hymen before your wedding day if it's still intact. Now you may have done this already by using internal sanitary tampons or by practising putting a diaphragm cap in place. But if not you may like to try doing this: simply insert the tip of a finger into your vagina while lying on your back and gently push downwards towards your back passage. A few times prior to your marriage will be sufficient.

We suggest you take along one or two of those mini stick-on sanitary pads, just in case you have a little bleeding from your hymen after the first time. If you're worried about being too dry down below you could purchase a tube of K-Y Jelly from the chemist as well, though this is far from essential.

Of course, don't forget everything else! You won't have much fun if you leave the tickets behind in the other jacket or forget your passports. With all the hustle and bustle it's as well to make a list and check the items off before you leave.

Have you packed everything? Well, you might like to take this book with you. It could make interesting bedtime reading together! But above all, pack your love, your hopes, desires and expectations. The Lord is going to bless your union and there's no reason why you shouldn't have a superb time together that will set you on course for a lifetime of joyful love-making.

6

The First Time

Let's assume you've arrived at your hotel early evening. You dump your bags, fall into each other's arms and breathe a sigh of relief. Alone together at last. And about to make love. You're ready to enter the true mystery of sexual union. 'A man will leave his father and mother and be united to his wife, and they will become one flesh' (Genesis 2:24).

If you're both virgins this will be one of the most holy moments of your lives. And even if you're not, provided you've brought your lives into the plan of God as we outlined in the first chapter, he is still going to make this a supremely precious occasion. The first time you make love together as husband and wife.

So, what should you do now?

It all depends on your mood really. There is no 'correct' procedure for your wedding night, no 'proper technique'. But there are quite a lot of things you can do to guarantee a successful beginning to your married love-life.

You have two main options before you. If you're both raring to go then you can make love straightaway. You may like to follow that by sharing a bath together. Perhaps then you could go and have something to eat, maybe a stroll, and if you wish, make love again when you go to bed for the night.

On the other hand, you may prefer to unwind a little first. Go for a walk, have an evening meal or just visit the local burger bar. Then come back and make love. You can go straight to sleep after that. Or take a bath. It's up to you. By the way, having a bath or shower isn't necessary after you've had intercourse; it's not unclean or anything like that. It's just that a bath will help you relax after such a long and demanding day—and it's such an enjoyable way of getting to know one another!

Whenever you decide to make love you'll want to be uninterrupted—so put the 'Do not disturb' sign on the door and make sure it's locked.

Try to set the right mood. There will be times when you'll make love with all the lights blazing and other occasions when it'll be fun groping in the dark, but we reckon soft, low lighting is best for this night. If you can get some romantic music on the radio as well, it'll help.

If you're using a cap and spermicide it's best if you insert this in the privacy of the bathroom on this occasion. You probably won't worry about it once you've settled into married life but you may find it a bit embarrassing at first.

You may like to undress each other completely on this first night. This can be a very pleasant introduction to each other's nakedness. You can do this best standing up. But take your own tights off first, and remove your own shoes and socks. Struggling with these does rather spoil the effect.

Kiss and cuddle while you're doing this. Don't rush. It's especially important that you tell your bride how beautiful she is. She may be more self-conscious than you, but even if she isn't she'll still appreciate the security of knowing you find her so attractive. These things matter to a woman, so be generous with your praise. And, both of you, have a good giggle now and then, especially when zippers get stuck!

Alternatively, you may wish to don that nightie and lounge seductively on the bed, or make an entrance from the bathroom. The choice is yours. What we suggest you *don't* do is to hurriedly undress with your backs to each other and then dive beneath the sheets. Like Adam and Eve you should be naked and unashamed in each other's presence. Start how you mean to continue.

Perhaps now, or just before you undress, you might like to take the opportunity to give thanks to the Lord for his goodness towards you and ask him to bless your love-making. It's a great pity that some Christians have set sex over and against their spiritual lives. We trust you'll never think like that but will be glad to have the Lord in your bedroom and his loving presence blessing your sexual union. Tell him you are ever so grateful for this glorious gift which he has bestowed on you.

You have now a complete freedom to make love but, as the man, you need to be careful not to go wild! There's a very real difference between the way men and women get aroused sexually and if you don't appreciate this, your wife is going to be a very disappointed woman. The Bridegroom in the Song of Songs understood it when he said to his new wife, 'You are a garden locked up, my sister, my bride; you are a spring enclosed, a sealed fountain' (Song of Songs 4:12). You have to unlock the garden and release the fountain. That takes time and consideration as you begin to arouse her in preparation for intercourse. It's no use plunging straight in, if you'll pardon the expression! You see, you get aroused very quickly and come down just as rapidly when it's over. She climbs slowly and declines gently afterwards. Respect that fact and you'll become a good lover.

If we draw a simple graph to illustrate this you'll understand what we mean. (See overleaf.)

It's easy to remember: the breast shaped curve is hers; the somewhat penis-shaped one is yours. The idea is that you should both peak at the same time and that means you have to begin arousing your wife while holding yourself back because you just don't need so long. What follows will help you to start right.

Once you're both completely naked go lie on the bed— that's more comfortable than the floor for the first time. As you lie side by side, begin gently to caress one another's bodies, but avoid your sexual organs at this stage. Although

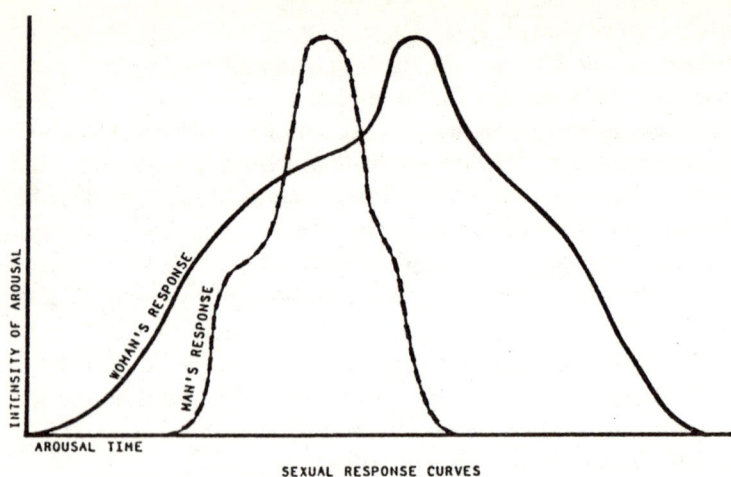

SEXUAL RESPONSE CURVES

you won't go too far wrong by letting your hands follow their own course, we recommend that you read the chapter entitled 'Opening Caresses' for some detailed advice on foreplay.

Love talk is an important part of your sexual fellowship. Women are generally more turned on by what they hear than by what they see. We reckon this goes back to Adam and Eve. Adam *saw* Eve and was captivated by the sight. Eve *heard* Adam as he expressed his appreciation of who she was. So do continually tell your bride how gorgeous she is and how much you love her.

This is how the Lover speaks in the Song of Songs. (Though it may have been the woman's girl friends watching her dance naked or flimsily clad. Either way she hears her beauty admired.) We've given the most probable translation.

> How beautiful are your sandalled feet, O prince's daughter! The curves of your thighs are like jewels, the work of a skilled craftsman. Your vulva is a rounded goblet that never lacks blended wine. Your belly is a mound of wheat encircled by lilies. Your breasts are like two fawns, twins of a gazelle. Your neck is an ivory tower. Your eyes are the pools of Heshbon.... How beautiful you are and how pleasing, O love, with your delights! (Song of Songs 7:1–4, 6).

Get the general idea? You might not manage his poetic imagery but do your best in plain English!

At some point your wife should roll onto her back, bend her knees and spread her thighs. The Song of Songs will give you the picture: 'His left arm is under my head, and his right arm [caresses] me' (Song of Songs 2:6). This is the time for your hand to wander down her body, until you reach her vulva where you can begin to lightly caress the whole area.

For a sexually inexperienced woman the clitoris is the one focus of arousal and she won't reach an orgasm unless it's well stimulated. So, after a while begin to concentrate your caresses near the top where the clitoris is, using a light circular movement. As her arousal increases, the lips of her vulva will swell and you'll be able to slide your fingers into the groove. This will be moist if you're doing things right and you can use this moisture to caress her clitoral area. Don't go too hard or let this bit get dry or else it becomes irritated. Ask her how she feels and whether you're getting it right. She may want you to go faster or slower, harder or softer.

Her own hands shouldn't be idle during this period. You'll find it particularly pleasurable if she strokes your inner thighs, your back and buttocks, and lightly caresses your testicles.

It'll soon be apparent that your wife is becoming quite aroused. You'll know this by her quickened breathing and because she's beginning to writhe a bit, as well as being moist down below. 'You are a garden fountain, a well of flowing water' (Song of Songs 4:15). You should now slip the tip of one finger into her vagina. Incidentally, you should ensure beforehand that your fingernails are evenly trimmed so as not to scratch her delicate membranes. Don't stab your finger in but glide it in from above and gently press down on her hymen, assuming it's still intact. At the same time keep the motion going on her clitoris. The idea is to stretch the hymen a little so as to make actual penetration a bit easier.

At this point, a wife should take hold of her husband's erect penis and gently massage it, but avoid the head. If you're using sheaths then this is the time to slip one on. You should have this unpacked beforehand. If you are not using a sheath we recommend you apply some saliva to his penis with your fingers, especially making sure that the underside near the base is well lubricated. If you prefer, you can use K-Y Jelly. In which case you need to have the tube to hand and to have already punctured the seal with the pointed cap. Strange stuff is K-Y Jelly; it always seems to be the coldest thing in the room. So you might like to warm the tube on a radiator or under the hot tap beforehand, if you think of it!

Your husband should also apply some saliva or gel to your vulva particularly around the vagina. You only need a small amount, about the same as a squirt of toothpaste. Spermicidal jelly will serve as an alternative if you're using a cap. (K-Y Jelly is not a contraceptive, incidentally.)

Well, you are ready to become truly one flesh. It's the moment when a woman can say, 'Let my lover come into his garden and taste its choice fruits' (Song of Songs 4:16). Or, more colloquially, 'I want you.' Already you're lying in the right position. Get your husband on top of you and between your spread thighs but with his arms extended so that you are not in actual bodily contact. Then take hold of his penis and direct it into your vagina—you may have a little difficulty finding it but you'll manage if he doesn't shove.

Once he's in position get him to push gently forwards and down at about 45° while you rock your pelvis up to meet him. He'll know he's on course because he'll feel the tightness of your hymen on the underside of his penis. As soon as the head is inserted he should slowly slide the rest of it in and at the same time bend his arms until your bodies are in complete contact. But get him to support his weight on his forearms— you don't want to be crushed! If you are a virgin you're bound to feel a little discomfort as your hymen stretches and breaks but that will be mingled with the intense pleasure of receiving your lover into your body. Hug him tight. If you follow this properly there's no need for it to be absolute agony at all.

He'll want to begin thrusting at once but there's value in him remaining still just for a few moments while you, with a gyrating motion of your hips, rotate your clitoris against the base of his penis. This will get you going again and allow him to acquire control of himself before commencing the action. You are not to be passive—don't 'lie back and think of England' but enthusiastically meet your husband's thrusts with your own. You have quite as much to give as he does.

It won't be long before the pace of your intercourse speeds up and your husband will race towards his climax. As he does, and he can let you know by gasping, 'I'm coming,' press up hard against him. You may by doing this reach an orgasm yourself.

A husband will know if his wife gets there, because she'll pant and gasp and maybe cry out, certainly her whole body will stiffen. It's not so easy for an inexperienced woman to reach an orgasm on the first night as it is for you. So try to help her. As soon as you've come, your penis will begin to shrink, but don't withdraw at once. Allow her to rotate her clitoris against you so that she can come to a climax. Too many couples give up too soon. The fact that you have done does not mean it's all over and the opportunity is lost for her. With experience, you'll probably learn how to reach orgasm simultaneously almost every time but at the moment you'll need to give her a little more time and attention—but that's what love is all about.

Alternatively, and particularly if you're using a sheath, you may roll off her and continue to caress her clitoral area with a firm rapid circling motion of your fingers while embracing her. She may then reach orgasm. In fact, a woman is quite capable of having one orgasm after another— something men can't do. But don't continue if she feels sore.

As you wind down continue to caress one another gently and lovingly. Now is the moment to say thank you and to encourage each other that you were both good. Everyone feels a bit insecure about their first time, so be reassuring to one another. Give thanks to the Lord also.

All being well, you'll both be left with a warm glow in your loins and a sense of tremendous satisfaction. Depending on your plans you can either share that bath together or just sink into blissful well-earned sleep.

> I have come into my garden, my sister, my bride; I have gathered my myrrh with my spice. I have eaten my honeycomb and my honey; I have drunk my wine and my milk (Song of Songs 5:1).

7

Hitches

There's often a conflict between what actually takes place in life and what we would ideally like to take place. A large part of the art of loving is coping with the reality while still aiming for the ideal. For example, you may ideally like to win a marathon; in reality you usually come last. So you have to be a bit philosophic about it, have a laugh—and then get out there training so that you come one from last the next time. You're on your way to your dream.

It's the same with love-making. We've just described how to do it successfully the first night—and you may get it just right; the perfect honeymoon. But things don't always work out quite as we would wish.

For a start you may arrive later than you expected. The car might break down on the way or you run into the traditional British 'motorway maintenance' hold-up. Planes can be delayed for an unbelievably long time.

The hotel room may not be quite as the brochure described it: 'What, single beds? We asked for a double.' 'Sorry, Senor, but that is all we are having.' There may be no bath, no restaurant, not even a nearby chip shop! You need what military experts call 'a flexible response to the situation'. You'll only be disappointed if you hang on to your original ideas.

Then your love-making itself may go a bit awry. That

seductive attempt to undress one another may turn out to be more a case of jammed zippers, impossible bra clips and buttons flying everywhere! Let alone falling flat on your face as you try casually stepping out of your dropped trousers. You've got to laugh. It's no use ever taking yourselves too seriously, but least of all when you try to make love. God doesn't want you uptight about it.

Contraceptives, particularly sheaths can be quite hilarious. Assuming you've not forgotten to bring them anyway, you can puncture the first one accidentally, have the second fly off the end as you try to put it on, and lose your erection by the third. Just relax and try again in a few minutes.

Or premature ejaculation may be the difficulty—your husband coming too quickly to his climax. We'll tell you how to overcome that problem later in chapter 11. It's just that some men get so tensed up that the first physical contact with their wives causes them to ejaculate. It could happen as soon as you caress his penis. Or as he tries to enter you. Maybe just a few seconds later. He'll feel a failure and you'll be left high and dry. But don't despair. There's an alternative.

He can still bring you to orgasm simply by applying a little lubrication to your clitoral area and massaging it for a while. Perhaps he might slip a finger into your vagina and rub both parts at once. You can guide him as to what you find best.

Of course, you may just commence your period on the wedding day. It happens! That will probably rule out intercourse for you. So, stimulate one another by hand. All you need to do, is to hold the shaft of your husband's penis with your fingers and massage it up and down until he reaches climax. A few handy tissues will mop up his ejaculate.

Some sex manuals actually recommend that you bring one another to orgasm by hand on the first night instead of attempting intercourse. This has the advantage in letting you observe one another's sexual responses as well as more or less guaranteeing some success. It's up to you. Only if you do decide on this, it's better that your husband brings you to orgasm first because he'll be apt to lose interest if it's the other way round.

This practice of bringing one another to orgasm by hand is a perfectly acceptable way of sharing love together particularly on those occasions when intercourse is not feasible, for example, during periods or mild vaginal infections. There's no need whatsoever for any guilt feelings about it being dirty or unnatural. It isn't.

To be honest, a lot of women don't reach orgasm during their first act of intercourse. That doesn't mean they're undersexed or frigid. Experience will soon prove otherwise. So don't worry if you don't quite make it. If you follow our suggestions in the previous chapter you'll still have a very enjoyable and satisfying time. Don't forget, practice makes perfect. There's always tomorrow. Or tonight. You can take that bath and try again later when he's slowed down a bit and you're more relaxed yourself.

Should you arrive at your honeymoon destination very late and you are both absolutely shattered, we recommend you forget about 'the first night' altogether. Go to sleep and have a try the next morning. You'll find it much better.

Speaking of the next day reminds us that you generally make love more than once on a honeymoon! As a woman you may feel a little sore on the second or third occasion. There are three things that can cause this. The first is the localized soreness of your torn hymen. Then you may have some aching muscles down below. And, thirdly, you might be slightly bruised—particularly around your clitoris. After all, you aren't used to all this battering, are you? Just tell him to go a bit more gently the next time. It doesn't take long to get used to things.

The worst that might happen is that you get a touch of honeymoon cystitis. This is sometimes caused by a bruising of the urethra which allows bacteria to invade your waterworks. The symptoms are a burning pain upon passing urine and an ache in your lower back or belly. If it occurs, drink as much water as you possibly can in order to flush the germs out; say, half a pint every twenty minutes for three hours and at frequent intervals after that. Visit a doctor if it doesn't clear up in a day or so. See also under Appendix One.

All being well you won't be much the worse for wear the next day and you can make love as often as you like, morning, noon and night, if you want. Some couples hardly leave their bedroom! Be flexible to each other's needs and desires.

This is a time of wonderful discovery. You can if you wish more or less follow the pattern of the first night on subsequent occasions, but now that your virginity is dealt with, you can begin to experiment and broaden your sexual experience. The next section of this book will give you some good ideas.

Finally, whatever your first night is like, if you show care and consideration for each other, if you set out to do one another good, by whatever means, you'll have a super time away together with plenty of laughs, much romance and lots of pure pleasure. 'Eat, O friends, and drink; drink your fill, O lovers' (Song of Songs 5:1).

THE ART OF LOVE-MAKING

All artists need a measure of inspiration, coupled with good technique and a lot of perseverance. In this section we seek to provide encouragement in each of these qualities as we develop the theme of creative love-making.

It is an art. Although there are basic skills worth learning, sexual intercourse is much more than just a matter-of-fact encounter. Hence, our aim in what follows is not to provide 'a method for satisfactory sex' but rather to stimulate couples into developing an imaginative and fulfilling love-life which is uniquely their own.

It all starts with two newly-weds who've just completed their first few brush strokes....

8

Setting the Scene

Honeymoons don't last for ever. Too soon we find ourselves back in the hurly-burly of life; commuting to and from work, doing the household chores when we're dog tired, late-night shopping, decorating the flat and trying to make the money stretch until pay day. But there's always sex as a consolation prize—that is, if you've any time, energy, or even desire left at the end of it all!

One of the discoveries we made early in our marriage is that you can't make love in a vacuum. (Perhaps it's the shortage of air!) Or to put it another way, the quality of your sex life is determined by how you live the rest of your life together. The idea that all you need is a good bedroom technique is a false one. Practising twenty different positions, knowing all the erogenous zones and doing it in every room of the house will be of no avail if you don't learn how to live together in harmony. This is the reason why so many marriages fail today.

As Christians you have a tremendous start. You know your marriage is in the will of God, he's in control of your lives, you're surrounded by a supportive family—and the grace of God makes you very loving people. But you can still be in for a few shocks. Former independence dies hard and adjusting to your partner's way of doing things can be quite a painful process—especially when you just *know* your way is better!

The first year of marriage is when much of this adjustment needs to take place. For this reason we'd recommend that you don't allow work, church commitments or leisure time activities to squeeze out the time you require for building your relationship. God made special provision for newly-wed Israelites to get properly acquainted when he decreed:

> If a man has recently married, he must not be sent to war or have any other duty laid on him. For one year he is to be free to stay at home and bring happiness to the wife he has married (Deuteronomy 24:5).

Interpreted into our modern context this means spending as much time together as possible, sharing your activities, talking through the difficulties—and laying the foundations of a really good sex life.

You'll find your finest sexual enjoyment takes place when you're both in a relaxed, cheerful and spontaneous mood. This happy state is by no means automatic and you have to take positive steps towards achieving it. We've found that the three main hindrances to this consist of unresolved conflicts, tiredness and lack of stimulus. So it may be helpful to consider each of these issues in turn.

Unresolved conflicts

It comes as quite a jolt to most newly-weds when they have their first row. Somehow all the romantic ideals and the vows seem shattered in the flurry of angry words, banged doors and shed tears. The actual cause may be anything. It's likely to be over money, or the in-laws, or because one of you got in late and the other was worried sick. It may be the clothes lying all over the floor, lack of a clean shirt, burnt toast or failing to help with the washing up.

Let's say straightaway that it doesn't mean you've made a terrible mistake in getting married. What's happening is quite normal and, if you handle things correctly, you'll be closer to one another when it's over. Living together exposes us to both the beauties and the blemishes of our characters as never before. We face reality—and that's a good thing because true love is not blind, and nor should it be.

So one of the first steps to harmony is to accept each other as you are—complete with flaws. No one should enter marriage like the bride who was heard muttering as she made her entrance, 'I'll alter him.' (Actually she was trying to remember the order of events—aisle, altar, hymn!) You need an attitude which says, 'I'm prepared to be changed by my partner.'

The second thing is to resolve your conflicts quickly. All our married life we've followed Paul's counsel, 'In your anger do not sin. Do not let the sun go down while you are still angry, and do not give the devil a foothold' (Ephesians 4:26). This means never going to sleep without saying sorry and forgiving each other. Mind you, to be honest the sun has got pretty low on the horizon on occasions and we've gone to bed quite grim! But then neither of us has been able to sleep and we've always put things right.

'Be kind and compassionate to one another, forgiving each other, just as in Christ God forgave you' (Ephesians 4:32). As women are often more hurt by rows than men we believe the husband should take the initiative in apologizing. The rights and wrongs of the issue aren't so important. What matters is that you're out of fellowship. That must be restored as soon as possible. The lesser problem can be solved tomorrow if necessary.

If you build this into your marriage a conflict will never become a problem. You'll maintain a genuine oneness of heart. And that will make your sex life what it's really meant to be—the highest expression of unity.

All in all it's better to have matters out in the open, even if that proves painful. You don't want any simmering resentment or frustration to mar your marital bliss for months on end when a bit of honest confrontation could have resolved it quickly.

Tiredness

Constant fatigue seems to be a permanent feature of many lives in this hectic modern society. It can ruin your love-life. Yet an awful lot of exhaustion can be avoided by paying a bit of attention to your lifestyle. For example, watching television can not only keep you up too late but the tiring bombardment of images upon your mind may make restful sleep hard to come by. There's a lot to be said for not owning a television set in the early years of your marriage. You need to talk a lot—and we all know it's the great conversation killer.

Then there's the constant round of meetings and other church activities which can sap your energies. Please don't misunderstand us. For many years we've served the Lord enthusiastically and have encouraged others to do the same. But we're addressing you as a newly-married couple seeking basic sexual adjustment and we want to advise you to be careful about how many commitments you take on, especially during your first year together.

It's better to do a few things well than to run yourselves into the ground through a multitude of activities to the detriment of your private and sexual life together. And watch the lateness of the hour also. Very little is generally achieved in meetings which drag beyond 9:30–10:00 p.m. unless it's something special. Don't be afraid to leave early so that you can minister your love to each other. That's not being unspiritual—and maybe your leaders will get the message, too!

The other major cause of tiredness is sheer overwork. You may, of course, have a very demanding form of employment which you can do little about, but we're thinking more of those things you can control. For instance, there's the decorating, building cupboards and shelf units, conquering that wilderness jokingly called a garden. Everyone likes the idea of having all these tasks finished, but life isn't really like that. It's actually an ongoing process. So it's a bit pointless driving yourselves into the ground over such things, because there's always something else to be done. Generally speaking you've plenty of years over which to do it all and you can afford to plan the work out sensibly.

What we'd like to suggest as a good pattern for the early months of your marriage is that you're always home with enough time left to wind down from the day. You may wish to do that by cuddling up on the sofa for half an hour with soft music and drinking chocolate. Perhaps you prefer to go straight to bed and chat for a while in each other's arms before making love. Whichever way suits your style best, make it a feature of your life. This may involve politely sending friends on their way, leaving a bit early or calling a halt to the decorating at a reasonable hour, but we think you'll find it worth while. Of course, if you work nights or shifts you'll have to adjust your plans accordingly.

Lack of stimulus

This may seem a strange reason to give for unsatisfactory sexual adjustment in early marriage. After all, here you are in the prime of life, and with all the freedom you could wish for. Yet many young brides don't enjoy the earth-shattering experiences the books promise, and even some men grow uninterested because something seems to be missing in their sexual relationship. What it boils down to is a lack of adequate stimulation. We're not thinking at this point about the foreplay immediately prior to intercourse so much as about what goes on throughout the day.

If you're intending to make love at 10:30 p.m. you really need to begin at 7:00 a.m.—or whatever time you wake up. You can commence a long, slow process of arousal by finding time for a kiss and cuddle, a little intimate fondling and a few brushing caresses. You might like to whisper some suggestive ideas. It's amazing how much the husky promise of 'later, darling' can brighten up an otherwise dull day!

There's no reason why romance should cease once you're married. In fact, it ought to increase. So rather than taking one another for granted, we'd like to encourage you to continue the wooing process. Phone one another, meet for lunch if you can, buy your wife some flowers from time to time. Even write love letters if you wish. Arrange to meet somewhere after work and eat out before going on to a show.

The spirit of encouragement needs to permeate your marriage. We live in a verbally destructive society and we must not only guard against that infiltrating our relationships but take positive steps in building up one another. Compliment your wife on her appearance and character. Admire her beauty. Express appreciation for the way she cares for you and especially how good she is in bed—a woman needs to know this. Kind, encouraging and appreciative words from the heart are one of the best stimulants you can give to your wife.

Tell your husband how glad you are that he's the man who loves and protects you. Say what his love-making does for you. When you think a good thought about him, express it. And we've yet to come across anyone who is really tired of hearing their partner say, 'I love you.' The more you encourage each other's sense of personal worth the more confident you'll be in giving yourselves sexually.

As well as affecting us emotionally, love-making involves all our physical senses—sight, touch, sound, smell and taste. It's important then to stimulate all five in your partner. B.O., bad breath, an unshaven chin, face packs, curlers and holed tights do very little to encourage sexual ardour. But even at the end of a busy day a little consideration can make a lot of difference—perhaps a quick shower, a shave, a fresh dab of perfume or aftershave. More blatant hints and caresses during early evening will prepare you for later—or maybe you won't want to wait that long!

Although it's usual for the man to commence the advances with kisses, cuddles and love-talk, there's no reason why a woman should look upon herself as the sexually passive partner in a marriage. You shouldn't be afraid to take the initiative. After all, it was the girl who issued the invitation in the Song of Songs: 'Let him kiss me with the kisses of his mouth.' Your husband will be delighted if, on occasions, *you* seduce *him*.

Incidentally, although you'll both grow familiar with every intimate inch of your naked bodies it's worth a girl remembering the value of subtlety in the art of seduction, especially visually. By all means run around in the nude in your flat but you may well find that it's the see-through nightie, the saucy exposure of a breast when he's not expecting it, going braless, or letting the bathrobe slip and so forth, which will turn him on more effectively much of the time. Indeed, you might like to purchase a few particularly enticing garments for his eyes only. But make sure nobody's going to call!

What we've been seeking to get across is that you must think about love-making long before you go to bed; your 'seduction routine' needs to be built into your entire life together. Unless that happens you can never hope to attain the real heights of sexual satisfaction. However, practice all-day-seduction and you'll find, when you want to have intercourse, that both of you are easy to arouse because it's a natural extension of the stimulus you're already experiencing. You've trodden the foothills, the mountain-tops are in sight.

This brings us to the question of how often you should make love. As with everything else people's appetites vary, so it's best to ignore the national average and find your own norm. We'd like to recommend that you be guided by Paul's counsel:

> The husband should fulfil his marital duty to his wife, and likewise the wife to her husband. The wife's body does not belong to her alone but also to her husband. In the same way, the husband's body does not belong to him alone but also to his wife. Do not deprive each other except by mutual consent and for a time, so that you may devote yourselves to prayer. Then come together again... (1 Corinthians 7:3–5).

We strongly believe that if one of you is in the mood then the other should be willing to have intercourse. You should never allow sexual frustration to build up in your loved one. It's not only cruel but it exposes your partner to the temptations of adultery. At the same time loving consideration on the part of the one who wants to have intercourse should mean that on occasions he or she leaves it until another time. Marriage requires give and take—but mostly give!

It's quite common for a husband to be the one who most needs sexual release, especially early in marriage. This is partly biological due to the continuous production of sperm and partly caused by the stronger psychological urge in men. On the other hand, as a young wife, though you may obtain considerable sexual satisfaction through intercourse, your fully-fledged desires will not have yet matured. In fact, most women don't reach their real peak of sexual yearning and fulfilment until their late thirties.

The key to a woman attaining sexual maturity lies in her regularly responding to her husband's initiatives; his passion ignites hers. So it's in both your interests that you always offer to make love if he so desires. In fact, you should be proud of your ability to satisfy your man and with this attitude of loving service you'll never feel used by him.

Practically speaking, we would suggest that every night you make yourself available and have some exploratory love play just to see if either of you is in the mood. If one of you is, then make love. On most occasions you'll both reach orgasm even if one of you wasn't full of passion at the start.

This will probably mean that you make love considerably more often than the national average. But we believe that's a good thing! Not only is there nothing wrong with having intercourse most nights of the week but it's actually beneficial to your relationship. Find your own level by experience. You've nothing to 'live up to', just to yield yourselves to one another in love as often as it pleases.

Of course, for a few days each month a wife will have her period. Most couples find intercourse too messy at this time and prefer to abstain. This can present a few problems particularly if, say, the husband is away on business at the wrong time or the couple are relying on the rhythm method of contraception. It may mean that they are not able to make love often enough for their needs. Although intercourse during the heaviest part of the period may be impractical, what about at the beginning or towards the end?

Under the Jewish law a woman was ritually unclean for seven days from the commencement of her period and any man having intercourse with her made himself unclean for seven days (Leviticus 15:19, 24). This uncleanness of women was part of the curse of the Law. But that is lifted by Christ who became cursed for us on the cross. One benefit is that women are freed from any stigma or inferiority because of their sex. 'There is neither Jew nor Greek, slave nor free, male nor female, for you are all one in Christ Jesus' (Galatians 3:28). A woman is then no longer ritually unclean for seven days a month and that means there is no religious taboo against intercourse during this time.

As far as hygiene is concerned, that clearly had some bearing upon matters for a primitive society dwelling in a hot, desert situation where water was at a premium. Not being able to wash properly afterwards meant intercourse during menstruation carried some risk of infection. In our twentieth-century world of readily available soap and water, that risk need no longer exist.

Provided you're both happy about it, if you so desire and if there is no excessive bleeding which might indicate something wrong, you're at liberty to make love during periods. Some women actually find that the relaxation resulting from inter-course eases the discomfort at the commencement of men-struation. And a woman may find her own sexual desires quite high towards the end. With the simple hygiene measure of washing afterwards, love-making at this time can be very satisfactory for both partners.

What we've sought to do in this chapter is to show you how to create the right environment or context for your sex life. We hope we've communicated that making love is a full-time occupation and much more than a quick fumble under the sheets. With the grace of God your relationship will blossom into a lifetime of romance, passion and tender care which will make you truly 'one flesh'. And even if it's too much to ask that you be intoxicated with love all the time, at least we trust you'll never again be quite sober!

9

Opening Caresses

For a man to reach a climax during intercourse proves no more than that he's a normal male of the species. It takes much more than that to make him a good lover.

Through lack of knowledge and consideration many sexual encounters consist of little more than a few cursory fumblings, hastily followed by five minutes' frantic thrusting, all of which leaves the wife high and dry and wondering what the fuss was about in the first place. Such a boorish approach is well expressed in the blunt American phrase, 'Wham! Bam! Thank you, ma'am!'

True love-making, on the other hand, requires a measure of skill and thoughtfulness, a time for sensitively caressing one another as a preparation for intercourse. This is called foreplay. If it's done properly, it will more or less guarantee complete sexual satisfaction for you both.

In this chapter we would like to suggest some of the caresses which you can best incorporate into your foreplay. Rather than providing you with an exhaustive list we want to propose a basic approach. With a bit of imagination you'll soon create your own variations on the theme and it won't be long before you're quite accomplished lovers. If you do find us saying the obvious at times that's only because we've counselled so many who have been sexually frustrated for want of being told the obvious. We'd be doing a disservice by not being specific.

It's usual to begin by describing the erogenous zones, by which we mean those parts of our bodies which are particularly sensitive to sexual stimulation. However, we'll return to these in a moment, because actually the most important erogenous zone you have is your mind. No amount of physical caressing will make up for a lack of attention to your thoughts, feelings and imagination.

In the previous chapter we tried to stress the value of cultivating a relaxed and positive spirit in your relationship. As far as possible your actual love-making should commence with a time of putting one another at ease. You may do this at the end of a busy day, for example, by simply embracing in bed for a while and chatting over the events of your day or praying together. Communing like this is part of the business of making love.

This should naturally lead on to some expressions of tenderness and here we'd like to emphasize the importance of visual and verbal caresses. Even a superficial reading of the Song of Songs tells us that the lovers used their eyes and mouths to great effect. Quite unashamedly they observe one another's naked bodies and describe in frank, vivid metaphors their respective charms. In the fourth chapter the man's eyes caress his beloved from her head down to her breasts. In the seventh he begins at her feet and allows his eyes to run slowly over her figure to the crown of her head before returning to her bosom. Not to be outdone, in the fifth chapter, she glides her eyes appreciatively over her man's nude form.

This combination of visual stimulation and verbal description is very important in building up your partner's sense of self-worth. You'll also find it stirs you sexually; frank mutual appreciation is one of the best aphrodisiacs in existence.

You may or may not be a very articulate person. If you're a poet then you can create your own versions of the Song of Songs, but if not you can still find ordinary words to express your endearment. Even: 'Cor, you don't half look scrumptious!' is better than nothing!

Another thing you might like to try is to describe what you're about to do to each other, or say it as you're actually doing it. This can be quite a turn-on. It also feeds the imagination and this contributes towards helping you not to fantasize about other men or women when you're making love—a problem which many people wrestle with in our adulterous society. We'll return to this in chapter 15.

Now, what about these physical erogenous zones? God has designed certain parts of our bodies so that the right caresses will arouse us sexually. It's actually a fair bit of us! Caressing the scalp, eyelids, ears, mouth, cheeks, sides of the neck, nipples, lower belly, the genitals, inner thighs, hands and the soles of the feet will work for both sexes. The nape of the neck, the small of the back and the buttocks are also particularly responsive in men, while the breasts, upper arm, the base of the spine and the back of the knees are additional areas of sensitivity in women.

Needless to say, we all vary enormously and you shouldn't consider yourself undersexed if you don't get turned on when a particular part of your body is caressed. For example, you may or may not have sensitive breasts; it could vary with the time of the month. Or you might find your ear being kissed too intense. Some days a particular stroke will get you going, another it may just tickle or irritate you. As your hands get used to exploring every inch of each other's bodies you'll perhaps find some surprising erogenous zones which aren't in any of the books. Happy hunting!

According to your mood you may be easy or difficult to arouse. With experience, your partner will gradually become sensitive to your varying needs. Sometimes just stroking your little finger will send you into paroxysms of pleasure and your whole body will feel like one great erogenous zone. You just never know—that's part of the variety and uniqueness of each one of us.

Speaking generally, it's best to commence your love play with gentle caresses of a slow, silky, rhythmic quality. The back of your fingers stroking the side of your wife's neck, for instance. Or her running her fingers through your hair. Let your hands flow lightly over your partner's body. Vary the rate and pressure and keep them moving from one erogenous zone to another; your hands should never be still. Sometimes your partner may prefer you to use a light scratching action rather than stroking. Tell each other what feels nice. Incidentally, you may find caressing with the palms of your hands rather than your fingertips is more stimulating for you. Try it.

It's natural to kiss a lot during this period of arousal. As most couples know how to kiss we're not going to insult your intelligence by telling you what to do, except to say that moistened lips and a relaxed mouth make it the most pleasurable. But you'll want to vary the action a bit with passionate tongue-entwined kisses interspersed with playful teasing pecks. And don't forget that you can caress your partner's whole body with your mouth. By planting kisses or by running the tip of your tongue across the skin you can evoke shivers of delight from your loved one. You'll get the same effect by blowing gently on the skin too.

Many couples find it convenient to lie side by side during this phase—or you might like to begin in a standing position. You could try hugging very lightly or brushing your naked bodies together so as to caress one another without hands, maybe with one of you positioned above the other with arms extended to take your weight. Later on you may adopt the classic Song of Songs position with the wife lying on her back, knees slightly bent and legs parted, while her husband embraces her with one arm and caresses her with the other— 'His left arm is under my head, and his right arm embraces [caresses] me' (Song of Songs 2:6). This is very comfortable but it isn't *the* authorized position. You don't need proof-texts for every action! Variety is the spice of love as well as of life.

Whether you begin this part of your love-making clothed or otherwise is up to you. Caresses which begin over clothes and then creep underneath can be very sensual. But there's a lot to be said for stripping right off (including socks!) at some time. Not only does this give you the greatest freedom for the physical act of intercourse but it says you are making your whole body unreservedly available to your partner—and this is how it should be. Prudishness about nudity should have no place in your love life, nor should an 'I can't be bothered to undress' attitude. Do, however, make sure the room is warm or you'll be wheezing something like, 'How I love the texture of your goose-pimpled skin,' through chattering teeth!

Of course, on occasions you may prefer to make love with some clothes on, for example, suspenders and stockings, a transparent sexily-cut negligee—even welly boots and a bomber jacket if that turns you both on! There's nothing kinky about dressing up a bit if that's your scene together, provided the garments themselves don't become the object of sexual arousal or essential before it can take place.

A woman's breasts deserve careful attention; your wife won't appreciate their being mauled. In fact, she'll probably enjoy it most if you begin with a very light stroking using your cupped hand. You may then wish to circle your fingertip around her nipple before gently rolling it between your finger and thumb. Don't pinch! Some women have more sensitivity in the milk ducts which are located just behind the nipple. You can stimulate these by taking the nipple and the areola (the coloured surrounding) between your fingers and thumb and using a slow milking action.

It's perfectly appropriate for a husband to kiss his wife's breasts. Try smothering them with kisses, or burying your face between them before running the moist tip of your tongue teasingly across her skin. You can twirl your tongue around her nipples and gently suck them. Later on you might take the whole nipple and areola into your mouth and suck more firmly to stimulate pleasure in her milk ducts. Let her guide you as to what she most enjoys.

Incidentally, nipples vary in size and type like everything else; there's no such thing as 'normal' and it's no use a woman worrying about them or her breasts in general. Make them freely available for your husband's delight and you'll be fulfilling 50% of God's purpose in giving you the ones you've got. As a woman you know full well that erect nipples don't necessarily mean you're sexually aroused. It may just be the cold air! In fact, as your excitement increases, your nipples will begin to be engulfed by the swelling of the surrounding tissues and might not look very erect at all. It might help if your husband knows this. By the way, remember he has nipples to and they may be very responsive to the same sort of caresses which he bestows on yours.

Fondling each other's sexual organs is a vital preparation for intercourse and, although we think it's a mistake to begin there, sooner or later your hands should find their way to the genital area. We came across a woman some years ago who had never experienced an orgasm simply because she had never allowed her husband to touch her 'down there'. To her it was 'dirty'. This inevitably meant she wasn't properly aroused when he entered her so he always reached his climax long before she was ready. Constant disappointment made her grow uninterested in sex and that had serious repercussions in the marriage.

Remember that graph showing the different arousal rates for men and women? At least some genital caressing is normally necessary if a woman is to experience orgasm. It also helps a man develop self-control so that he doesn't come to his climax too soon.

You'll probably find it easiest to assume the 'Song of Songs 2:6 position' and the husband can start by gently stroking the whole vulval area. It may help you to imagine that you are seeking to coax a flower into full bloom by your caresses.

In a young wife the sexual focus is entirely on the clitoris and this is where your attention should be directed. After some months other parts of the vulva become responsive and in a sexually mature woman the whole area responds to stimulus.

Because the clitoris is very sensitive it can also get sore so when you begin massaging that area it should be with a circular rolling motion of your fingers but without any frictional rubbing. It should go without saying that you ought always to keep your fingernails well trimmed in order to avoid injury to your wife's tender parts. After a short while the inner lips of her vulva will begin to swell apart and you can slip a finger into the groove. Various glands in and around the vagina produce a natural lubrication to ease intercourse. You should use this moisture by dipping your finger into your wife's vaginal entrance and applying it to the head of her clitoris. By repeating this process at intervals you can keep the clitoris moist, which will both heighten your wife's pleasure and prevent soreness.

Too much friction on the head of the clitoris will prove overintense for her so you should shift to rubbing the ball of your thumb alongside the clitoral shaft or using your fingers and thumb to massage the foreskin up and down the shaft. Vary this as suits her best.

As your wife becomes more sexually experienced the surfaces of her inner lips will become responsive and you can arouse her by rolling one between your finger and thumb or by light caresses with your fingertips using moisture from the vagina.

Your attentions should include the vagina. A finger can be inserted and with it you may mimic intercourse. After a couple of minutes you could add a second digit and give her some wiggly sensations. You may also find that the area just behind the entrance, the perineum, is particularly sensitive to some light caresses.

When your wife's inner lips are swollen so that the outer ones are pushed apart and the clitoris is engulfed, and when you can insert two fingers into a moist vagina, she is ready for intercourse. The flower is in full bloom. By now her breathing and heart rate will have increased and she may be flushed also. More important, she'll tell you she's ready.

Of course, a woman can easily be brought to orgasm by these caresses alone, particularly the clitoral ones. In fact, if she finds it difficult to get there during intercourse in the early weeks of marriage we recommend you to caress her to orgasm so that she can experience what it's like. You can also do this during her periods if she so desires.

Should you accidentally bring her to a climax before intercourse it doesn't mean it's all over. A woman is quite capable of having several orgasms at a time. But she'll need a few minutes of further preparation to regain her sexual excitement before you seek to enter her.

There are times when you'll find your wife isn't producing much natural lubrication. This may be due to hormonal fluctuations or she may be dry if she's just removed an internal tampon at the end of her period. It's vital that you supplement what she is producing if you are to avoid painful intercourse. You can do this either by transferring saliva from your mouth with your fingers or applying some K-Y Jelly, non-scented oil or spermicidal cream to her vulva. Some women react to saliva and if your wife does then rely on creams.

Although most men attain an erection easily enough— usually the moment love play commences—many worry about losing it. This fear can make a man hasty in seeking to prepare his wife, resulting in a lack of fulfilment for her.

No man in his prime need have this fear because even if he does wilt for a while, a wife who knows what she's doing can always bring him back to an erect state.

Your husband will appreciate you lightly caressing his scrotum and the shaft of his penis. In fact these soothing motions may help him contain himself. The actual muscle of his penis runs right between his legs behind the scrotum and you'll find that he enjoys you fondling him there. You can run your fingers from the base to the tip of his penis if you wish or you might like to grasp the shaft firmly and squeeze. Holding the shaft and massaging it up and down in a masturbatory manner he will find very pleasant—but not too much or else he may ejaculate early. Lightly running a fingernail up the underside is also stimulating for some men.

One possible way of firming up his erection if it's on the

wane is to grasp the shaft with one hand and hold the head between the thumb and fingertips of the other. You then give the head a sharp flicking twist a few times—but not *too* sharp! Actually almost any determined action on your part will get him going again.

The most sensitive part of your husband's penis is the connecting membrane (the frenulum) on the underside between the head and the shaft and the area just below it. You can tickle it or lightly scratch it and he will become very aroused. Because they are so stimulating these caresses should be reserved for the moment immediately preceding intercourse.

Find out what your husband likes best. With a bit of practice you'll be able to make his passion ebb and flow like the waves of an incoming tide on the seashore, each wave rising higher than the previous one, until you are ready yourself to receive his full flood.

As you both near the point of intercourse you'll find light caresses less stimulating. Firmer kneading of the more fleshy parts will arouse the deeper nerve fibres of your bodies, for example, grasping your partner's buttocks or using your clawed fingers to massage the back. Mild slapping, clutching and biting may enhance your pleasure because these actions send similar signals to your brain as those from your sexual organs during intercourse. We are not suggesting brutality, of course. You must do what your partner enjoys but that shouldn't ever involve real pain or physical damage.[1]

Quite a number of folk ask what we think about oral sex, that is, mouth to genital stimulation—*cunnilingus* when a man does it to a woman, *fellatio* when a woman does it to a man. Is it all right, or is it a perversion?

This is perhaps a good point to discuss what is or is not sexually acceptable as far as Christians are concerned.

---

[1] Sadism and masochism are deviant practices in which quasi-sexual pleasure is brought about by the inflicting and receiving of pain, respectively. Sexual satisfaction may prove impossible without the pain element being present. Specialist counsel is advised.

To begin, we must ask, 'What is a perversion?' Modern secular thinking is heavily conditioned by social surveys, and judges perversion not so much by whether an action is right or wrong in itself but by whether most people do it, approve of it or don't mind others doing it, provided no one gets unwillingly hurt in the process.

Christians approach the matter from an entirely different angle. We begin with God and his will for his creation. In so doing we find three criteria by which we may judge the rightness or wrongness of a sexual practice.

The first is: does it transgress the marriage covenant? 'Marriage should be honoured by all, and the marriage bed kept pure, for God will judge the adulterer and all the sexually immoral' (Hebrews 13:4). Adultery and all other forms of sexual behaviour which violate God's man-and-woman-one-flesh-for-life order are perversions. Multiple partners, animal sex, homosexuality, lesbianism, voyeurism, pornography, prostitution and flirtation are all examples of a distortion of God's plan.

The second criterion concerns practices which are contrary to God's natural order. Paul used this argument against homosexuality when he wrote,

> Even their women exchanged natural relations for unnatural ones. In the same way the men also abandoned natural relations with women and were inflamed with lust for one another (Romans 1:26–27).

There is a natural way of behaving which accords with the way God designed things to work.

Take anal intercourse as an example, whether between two men or a man and a woman. A vagina is clearly designed to receive a penis both for pleasure and reproduction. But what of an anus? Its apparent function is as a sphincter muscle to retain waste matter until a convenient time for us to void it. It can also be penetrated by a penis. But is it designed for this?

Arguments from design are seldom foolproof but we'd like to offer the following pointers:

The parts of our bodies always respond positively rather than passively to that use for which they were designed. A vagina to a penis. Our mouths when they eat and speak. Although it's possible to drink through one's nose, it's unpleasant because our noses aren't really designed for drinking. Anal intercourse is generally very uncomfortable, not to say downright painful, and a woman is unlikely to find it at all sexually satisfying because her back passage is simply not made for that purpose.

The obvious is usually right. You can eat with your feet, but it's hardly necessary or appropriate if you have hands. Why use an anus when a vagina is provided by the Lord?

Although things may go wrong through carelessness, weakness or accident when we use our parts according to their purpose, that use doesn't in itself cause harm. Damage is quite common in anal intercourse. The cells of the anus are, unlike those of the vagina, of a thin-walled type not at all suited to the friction of intercourse. So bleeding is common— this is how AIDS is transmitted among homosexuals. (AIDS is spread by other means, too—see Appendix One.) Also, repeated anal intercourse will stretch the sphincter muscle so that its proper function of bowel control is impaired. It is exceedingly unhygienic, too.

Anal intercourse between men and women is still illegal in Britain, though not between consenting adult males.

The third criterion for judging the validity of any sexual conduct is: how does it accord with self-sacrificing love? Paul says, 'Husbands ought to love their wives as their own bodies' (Ephesians 5:28). Anything which abuses your partner by the infliction of unwanted physical or mental suffering is perverse—it transgresses love. This doesn't mean you can't have a playful wrestle or a few fun slaps, but it does mean that inflicting pain as a stimulus to the tormentor is wrong, as is demanding that your partner participate in any practice which he or she finds distasteful.

The apostle John wrote, 'Perfect love casts out fear' (1 John 4:18). Many people enter marriage with various sexual inhibitions and personal taboos. Some of these can seriously hinder the relationship, like the woman we mentioned earlier who couldn't bear to be touched between her legs; others may be much less important, no more than legitimate likes and dislikes or natural shyness. Either way, the love of God must always determine our attitudes and actions towards one another.

If you truly love you will never force your desires on your partner; you won't nag, sulk, resort to emotional blackmail or use physical violence to get your own way. Instead, you'll exercise a patient, tender care towards your loved one which will for ever dispel from the mind any fear of being coerced into something which he or she finds emotionally or morally unacceptable. At the same time, your love will bring a healing to those areas of the personality which are genuinely in need of it.

The security of sharing God's love like this will release you into the freedom to do together what you really enjoy without any sense that you've necessarily got to do everything that can be done. That happy state is the will of God for all of us.

Whatever falls within these three guidelines is acceptable. If you both like swinging from the chandeliers, dressing up for sex, or acting out some seduction charades; if you prefer the kitchen table to the bed or brilliant lights and mirrors on the ceiling; if your thing is to caress one another with ostrich feathers; that's fine—provided you both enjoy it and you use your bodies as they were intended and within strict marital fidelity.

So, after all this, what about oral sex?

Evidently it is not an abuse of the marriage covenant. Nor does it distort design in so far as our mouths are made for kissing and all skin is responsive to kissing. When the woman cries for her lover's kisses in the Song of Songs, she doesn't specify which parts of her body he should kiss. So, in our opinion, oral sex is perfectly acceptable within marriage provided the vital third criterion is met, namely, neither partner feels forced into something he or she can't cope with.

Provided both of you want to try oral sex you should feel free to do so. It may become part of your love play, it may not. If one of you really doesn't like it then forget it anyway. Maybe in a few months or years it will come back into your love life. Perhaps it'll just become unimportant to you, as with many other things you might try together.

If you do decide to practise mouth to genital stimulation it makes sense to follow reasonable hygiene precautions. The slight risk of infection isn't so much to your mouths as to your sexual organs themselves. So you should clean your teeth and wash your private parts beforehand. You shouldn't indulge in oral sex if you have a cold or a mouth infection and especially if either of you has a cold sore around your mouth. If you become irritated by doing it anyway, you'd best leave it out of your foreplay.

Oral-genital caresses may develop from a succession of kisses down your partner's body or you may both adopt a head to tail posture, side by side or one on top of the other, legs parted—the so-called *soixante-neuf* or sixty-nine position.

A wife may like to kiss the shaft of her husband's penis. You can run your moist tongue along its length or swirl it around the head with the foreskin drawn back. You may perhaps take the organ into your mouth and gently suck while holding the shaft and using your tongue on the underside. You should never blow down the urethra as this can drive bacteria into the bladder and cause infection. We think you should normally avoid bringing your husband to orgasm this way as it rather defeats the object of foreplay. Though any sperm which may enter the mouth is quite harmless.

A husband may give his wife considerable pleasure by using his tongue on her vulva, particularly on her clitoris. You must keep your tongue moist and be careful how you do it otherwise she'll get sore. You may wish to very lightly chew on the clitoral shaft or suck one of the inner lips. If you want you could lap between her inner lips and down into her vaginal entrance. You must be careful not to scratch her with a bristly chin if you do this.

Oral sex can be a pleasurable part of your love play and may be a real help to a woman who finds it difficult to become aroused, but you must remember that of necessity it restricts conversation and eye to eye contact. So, in our view, it should constitute only a part and not the whole of your foreplay.

* * *

However you choose to prepare one another for intercourse the important thing is that you do it with loving care and consideration. Sexual intercourse is described in the Bible as 'knowing' your partner; it's the fellowship of your whole personalities and all your senses—and foreplay is a vital part of that communion.

We've sought to give you a few ideas and guidelines. You may already have found better ways of your own, or you may wish to adapt some of our suggestions. Experimenting together is part of the joyous discovery of your sexuality. You'll develop familiar caresses and with a bit of thought be for ever coming up with new surprises which will keep your marriage bed fresh. In the sensual imagery of the Song of Songs:

> …I will give you my love. The mandrakes send out their fragrance, and at our door is every delicacy, both new and old, that I have stored up for you, my lover (Song of Songs 7:13).

In the next chapter we'll talk about going through that door or, in our more prosaic day, making the connection.

IO

Making the Connection

Of all the human actions we perform, joining our bodies together for sexual intercourse is the most intimate. The two become one flesh and in that act of mutual possession you can truly say, 'I am my lover's and my lover is mine' (Song of Songs 6:3). But how best do you effect this exquisite union to make it all it should be? That's the theme of this chapter.

There comes a point in the course of your foreplay when you're ready to unite your bodies. If you've prepared one another thoroughly you'll both be brimming with urgent desire. The wife's vulva will be moist and fully opened. Her whole being will yearn to receive her husband. He'll have a firm erection and an irresistible craving to possess his wife. Neither can hold back any longer.

There are various ways of commencing intercourse. For example, you may keep your penis outside your wife's vagina for a minute or so and allow it to nestle between the inner lips of her vulva. You can tantalize her a bit by sliding the tip up and down the groove from her vaginal entrance to her clitoris and back again, maybe just dipping the head into her vagina. Or you may prefer slowly to slide in the full length of your penis at one go. Alternatively, you could enter her vagina with a series of short, ever-deepening thrusts. What you should try to avoid is simply thrusting it hard in, particularly if your wife has not been stretched by childbearing, as that could prove uncomfortable for her. You might miss, anyway, and she won't thank you for *that*! For this reason, it may be helpful early in marriage if she normally guides your penis in with her hand. She at least knows where the entrance is.

Just occasionally we've come across distressed couples who cannot manage normal intercourse because the wife finds the penetration unbearably painful. In fact, some marriages remain unconsummated for months and years on end for this reason. The condition is known as vaginismus and is due to a spasmodic contraction of the muscles surrounding the vaginal entrance so that the penis is shut out. The spasm can last for hours at a time and attempting intercourse will only make matters worse. The cause is almost always psychological; quite often the condition is triggered by memories of painful intercourse in the past, especially arising from rape, incest or brutal assault.

Under such circumstances it's no use a husband trying to batter the door down. That will only increase his wife's agony and sense of failure, as well as frustrating him. The couple need to talk through the underlying problems and pray for a healing of the emotional wounds. It will help greatly if an understanding minister or doctor can be confided in concerning the difficulty.

Meantime, they should not attempt to have intercourse but content themselves with loving caresses and bringing one another to orgasm by manual stimulation. As the wife grows more secure her husband can seek gently to stretch her muscles by inserting a finger into her vagina. When she can cope with this and do it herself, a second finger can be added—but any pain must be kept within tolerable levels. With patience, the problem can be overcome and the couple will enter the joys of normal intercourse.

Most women don't suffer from vaginismus and any pain felt upon penetration is usually caused by lack of adequate foreplay resulting in an unrelaxed vulva and dryness of the vaginal membranes. No wife is too small for her husband, however well-developed he might be. The vagina can stretch to allow a baby's head through and it lengthens naturally when a woman is aroused. A man with an exceptionally long penis *may* have to watch the depth of his penetration, but that shouldn't make the act itself painful.

Other possible causes of pain are infections and inflammations, a badly inserted diaphragm, soreness from a previous encounter, reaction to spermicides, or simply being approached at an odd angle.

Assuming all goes well and penetration isn't a problem you'll begin the natural thrusting motions of intercourse. It's tempting, particularly for a young man, to race to a climax with an energetic, rapid pounding of his poor wife, just hoping she'll keep up. Nine times out of ten she won't. So we'd encourage you to take your time savouring the act itself and not just the climax. Then even if your wife doesn't reach an orgasm on occasions she'll still feel very satisfied.

As soon as you've entered fully into her, try resting for a few moments. This will allow you to gain control of your urges. To keep her ardour burning without overstimulating yourself you can rotate the root of your penis (that is, your pelvic bone) against her clitoris. You might then commence some long slow thrusts, nearly withdrawing your penis each time. The slower you do this the longer your penis will feel to your wife—good for the male ego!—and she'll love it. This kind of control is easiest if you're positioned on top of her and supporting your weight on extended arms as though you were ready to do press-ups.

To maintain your wife's arousal you should keep yourself well up against her body so that your penis is pumping more or less up and down rather than forwards and backwards. This allows the shaft to slide in the vulval groove and create pleasurable friction upon her clitoris. Many a woman fails to be satisfied simply because her husband isn't at a steep enough angle. This approach is also best for a woman who hasn't had children because it doesn't stretch her too much. Once she's more experienced you can vary the angle much more.

Long slow strokes can be interspersed with short bursts of rapid thrusting either pressed hard up against her or using the full length of your penis. You might like to try a steady screwing action, too, by rotating your hips as you slide in and out.

Though the husband may initiate most of these movements a wife ought never to be passive in bed; she has a positive contribution to make during intercourse. You should rise enthusiastically to meet your husband's efforts and match his rhythm by vigorously rocking your pelvis. Alternatively, you can set the pace yourself. Some positions actually require that you do so. You may also want to vary the motion by gyrating your hips in a series of bumps and grinds like a belly dancer. It can be fun doing this to music!

There's no reason why with practice you shouldn't take twenty to thirty minutes or even longer enjoying intercourse in this fashion. You can talk, laugh, kiss and caress all the while and change positions as many times as you please. The wife can have one or two orgasms along the way if she likes. It all depends upon your stamina and your mood—and on the husband's ability to restrain himself. More about that in the next chapter, but one simple trick you can do if you feel you're losing control is, with your penis right in, to stop thrusting for a few moments and substitute the gyratory action, or just remain completely stationary.

You can use this opportunity to give your wife some extra thrills by twitching your penis. She can return the pleasure by squeezing you with her vaginal muscles. This is a similar action to the one you use to stop yourself urinating. In fact, when you next visit the loo practice stopping yourself for a few seconds in mid-flow to get the general idea.

Now, what about the various positions for intercourse? Take two jointed, padded structures of limited flexibility and connect them in the middle by means of one sliding joint in as many ways as you can conceive. Sounds like a Design and Technology project, doesn't it?

The gymnastic possibilities are almost limitless, provided

you combine the strength of an Olympic weight lifter with the agility of a contortionist. Yet even at a conservative estimate there are over seventy positions attainable by couples of average health and flexibility. Of course, they actually consist mostly of minor variations on a few basic ideas. You're unlikely to use anything like that number and, in practice, most people settle down to a few variations on two or three favourites. What you need are positions which are both sexually satisfying (you have to be able to move) and sufficiently varied so as to keep your love-making from becoming humdrum. So, rather than including every novelty, we've followed the advertiser's advice—'Try the rest, but here's the best.'

Though you can have intercourse standing up, this position is seldom very satisfying or practicable, especially if you're of differing heights. You may, nonetheless, like to try it at least once just to find out for yourselves. All the others fall into four main groups:

Husband on top

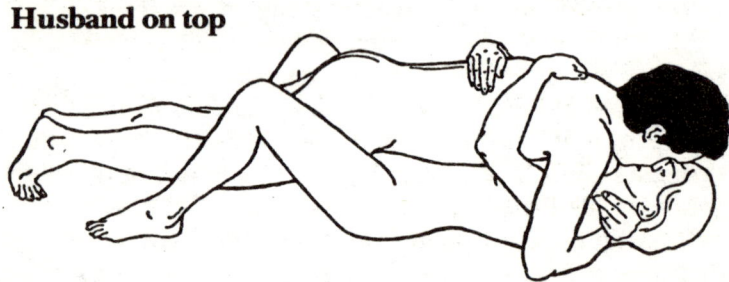

This is the most adaptable of all the positions and the favourite of many couples, being suited both to slow shallow intercourse and deep energetic thrusting. It provides a high degree of face-to-face intimacy and the good clitoral contact makes it the best position for mutual orgasm. For these reasons it's especially suitable for a couple to use during the early months of their marriage.

As a husband you'll need to ensure that your wife doesn't feel crushed under your weight in this position and we recommend that for most of the time you support yourself either on your forearms or by extending your arms straight. This latter variation allows you great control over your movements as well as a visual appreciation of your wife's face and breasts. It's also the best position if she's a back sufferer. However, your arms may begin to tire and you might, in any case, want a cuddle. So vary the posture. You could, for example, bend your arms so that your bodies just brush together. If your wife writhes a bit she can create some delicious sensations. When using this position, incidentally, you may prefer to have your feet pressing against something for leverage.

Other variations include your wife drawing her knees up to her chest so that you rest your torso on her shins. Or she may draw her legs up and wrap them around your waist with her ankles interlaced. If she's in a more athletic mood she could try hooking her calves over your shoulders so that you rest your body on the backs of her thighs and steady yourself with your extended arms. These positions tend to provide deeper penetration and the latter can particularly assist with conception.

However you choose to adapt this position it's probably best if you simply fall into a tight embrace as you both climax. In fact, whatever other positions they may use along the way this remains for the majority of couples the most satisfying way of finishing.

Wife on top

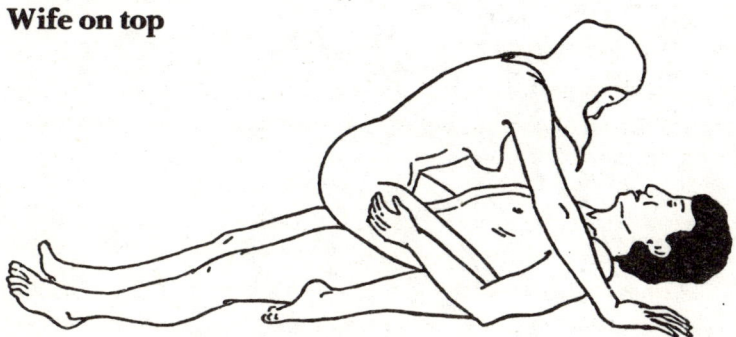

This is an excellent position, particularly if the couple are of very differing heights. It allows you as a wife great freedom in determining the rate and depth of penetration, but your husband has no need to feel passive as he can still meet your thrusts quite easily. Visually this position is very stimulating for him and he can fondle your breasts and clitoris without difficulty. Wife-on-top positions are ideal for the husband who suffers from back pain.

To adopt it you simply straddle your partner, take his penis and position it so that the head is just inside your vagina. You then lower yourself gently onto it. He should keep motionless until it's fully inserted.

You can try many variations. For example, you may lean forwards and embrace your husband. Or you might like to have your legs extended straight back outside his while you either support yourself on extended arms or cuddle him close. If you wish, you can use all these positions in reverse by simply turning around and facing his feet.

Another way of having the wife on top is for the husband to adopt a sitting or a kneeling posture, as in this example.

This adapts well if your husband sits on a chair or the corner of the bed and you straddle him placing your feet on the floor for leverage. Again you can vary these positions by facing away from him if you want.

Another modification is possible if you lie on your back with your bottom on the edge of the bed. Your husband kneels on the floor to enter you and you then wrap your legs around his body. It will work equally well if you decide to make love on the kitchen table with him in a standing position. Well, some people like to! Both this and the sitting posture are useful during pregnancy.

Side by side

These positions leave both partners without any weight on them and are particularly suitable if you want shallow penetration. You can obtain reasonably good clitoral contact and your hands are free for caressing. Talking and kissing are also easy.

You can vary this position by both lying side by side with your legs together or your husband can straddle one of your legs while you roll more onto your back. This increases the clitoral stimulation.

If you both lie on your sides facing the same direction your husband can approach from the rear. This is a very useful position during the later stages of pregnancy when the size of your tummy may make other positions difficult.

Side-by-side positions may be found easier in times of illness, tiredness or general debility.

Rear entry

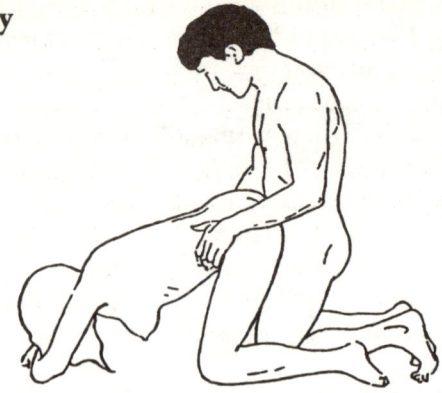

Rear entry doesn't mean anal intercourse, in case there's any confusion. This position is very suitable if your wife likes on occasions to adopt a submissive posture. It too is useful in the advanced stages of pregnancy and, more importantly, may significantly help conception if she has a retroverted uterus (that is, tilted backwards). Adapted so that she's kneeling on the bed and you're standing, this is a helpful posture if you suffer from back trouble.

Other variations include your wife being on her hands and knees or kneeling at the bedside with her body resting on the bed. As we've already mentioned, many other positions can be adapted for rear entry.

These forms of intercourse often provide deep penetration so it's important that you enter your wife with care. It's of considerable help in obtaining the right angle if she arches the small of her back downwards and juts her bottom upwards.

Although you have reasonable freedom to fondle your wife's breasts and clitoris, the obvious disadvantage of all rear-entry positions is the lack of face-to-face contact.

* * *

We hope this will give you some idea of the possibilities. You may be quite happy with what you do at the moment, of course, or you may like to experiment a little with some of our suggestions in order to broaden your horizons. You'll at least have some laughs—we hope no dislocations!—and you may just discover some delightful new methods to add to your store of love-making skills.

However you join your bodies, in the next chapter we'll talk about bringing your love to a blissful climax.

I I

Coming to a Climax

We simply couldn't help laughing the day one of our children came home and told us about the sex education lesson at school. The woman teacher had concluded the account by describing orgasm as 'a little tingle'. Whether she was herself sexually inexperienced, or even frustrated, we'll never know. Perhaps she was struggling with the inappropriateness of trying to teach sex in a classroom. Whatever her reasons, we hastened to assure our offspring that orgasm is very much more than a little tingle!

Sexual climax or orgasm is the most absolute of human experiences, a pleasure so intense that it almost hurts. Lovers gasp and groan as this fountain of sensual delight, this volcanic release of pent-up passion, erupts from the fusion of their bodies and sweeps them into an instant of irresistible ecstasy. The earth shakes—or at least the bed!

Then, as suddenly as it comes, it goes; the flood abates, passion subsides. It's as if the crashing exultations of the finale to the *1812 Overture* have been replaced by the gentle cadences of the *Pastoral Symphony*; peace, repose and a sense of well-being drift over the lovers as they lie healthily exhausted in each other's arms.

This is God's gift of orgasm. We hope you'll forgive us indulging in a bit of literary licence but we felt the theme deserved it!

We're aware that it's not like this for everybody. Sex is a let-down for a lot of people in our society and many don't enjoy even a little tingle let alone full-blooded orgasm. So, we'd like to talk about overcoming some of the common difficulties in this chapter, especially as they relate to the wife's satisfaction. Because male impotence is more likely to be a problem in later years we're leaving that to the last section of the book.

We'd also like to offer some advice on how to enjoy regularly a simultaneous orgasm and suggest one or two ideas to help heighten the experience for both of you.

Frigidity

No woman wants to be known as frigid but it's a sad fact that many wives go for years on end unable to experience sexual passion. Some dutifully submit to their husband's desires, though that's hardly satisfactory even for him—no man enjoys making love to a cold fish. Others refuse their partner altogether and finish up in separate beds.

Sexual disillusionment can easily lead to adultery and divorce, so it's vital to obtain help and deal with the root causes. These may lie within the wife herself, or they may be caused by a poor general relationship with her husband, or both may simply lack the correct skills in love-making.

People vary greatly in their responses to similar situations. One woman, physically abused by her father and later deserted by her husband, went on a sexual binge. Another girl, molested by her father, became totally frigid. In both cases it was a complex combination of repressed anger, fear and guilt which led to their extreme reactions.

Anger can easily block our finer emotional responses. Take the girl raised by a dominant mother and taught by her example to despise her father for his shortcomings. Not surprisingly, in adult life she found herself unable to respond to her husband. The anger which she had developed towards her dad now suppresses her ability to abandon herself in love towards her marriage partner.

The opposite is also true. A child who suffered at the hands of a dominant brutal father may grow into adulthood without having resolved the anger she feels towards him. One consequence can be sexual blockage.

Fear may make a woman frigid. It can be the simple fear of pain which may spring from the memory of rape, or it may be the subconscious fear of transgressing a parental taboo. If sex was a no-no subject in the family, and worse, if the girl was taught that no decent girl ever does that sort of thing (or at least if she does she must never enjoy it), then sex will always seem evil or dirty. Parents often have a lot to answer for when they make their children think sex is shameful.

Sometimes this taboo takes the form of religious guilt. Many times in its history has the church been marred by those who taught that sexual pleasure is the fruit of the Fall and, therefore, to be rejected by the truly spiritual. Nothing could be further from the truth! Sex outside of marriage is sinful, but within marriage it's a divine gift to be enjoyed to the full with thanksgiving. In fact, we'd go so far as to say it is wrong *not* to enjoy it within marriage. This is God's word on the subject:

> May your fountain [a symbol for sexual expression, ejaculation] be blessed, and may you rejoice in the wife of your youth...may her breasts satisfy you always, may you ever be captivated by her love (Proverbs 5:18–19).

> I delight to sit in his shade, and his fruit is sweet to my taste...I am faint with love (Song of Songs 2:3, 5).

The Lord invented sexual pleasure and intends us to enjoy it. If you are Christians your bodies are temples of the Holy Spirit, and that includes when you make love. By the Spirit, Jesus is present in your bedroom to bless your union. Religion that denies marriage and the enjoyment of sex is frankly demonic.

... things taught by demons... They forbid people to marry... For everything God created is good, and nothing is to be rejected if it is received with thanksgiving....' (1 Timothy 4:1, 3–4).

If you do find any remnant of guilt about sexual pleasure we recommend you talk it through with a Christian who has a good understanding of the liberty which the grace of God brings to our lives.

We've counselled a number of women who've been raped or molested, sometimes by a father, brother or other relative. Incest is far more prevalent in our society than most of us realize. Very often the girl will feel terribly guilty and the sense of shame may well block her sexual responses. It can be worsened if the relative apologizes because this may cause the girl to feel she led him on against his wishes. She may then hate her own body and her sexuality.

Let's set the record straight. Most girls don't go around 'asking for it'. If you were raped or the victim of incest it almost certainly wasn't your fault. You must face the fact that your father, or whoever, is guilty and is responsible for his own actions. Only when you've done this can you as a Christian choose to forgive him and so break the torment. Because of the prevalence of this problem we've included some additional counsel in Appendix Four.

Of course, some pre-marital affairs may well have been your own fault and the sense of guilt in that case is because you've actually transgressed God's law. The solution is honestly to acknowledge this and seek forgiveness. 'If we confess our sins, he is faithful and just and will forgive us our sins and purify us from all unrighteousness' (1 John 1:9). Confession of sin is also the key to cracking a difficulty to which we referred earlier, that is, when the thrill goes out of an already existing sexual relationship once the couple marry because it had been founded upon the excitement of secrecy and 'getting away with it' rather than on pure love. Repentance will bring renewal and restoration to your love-life, if that's been the problem.

We've been writing about serious and long-lasting frigidity with quite deep causes which often need specialist counsel. Not all lack of sexual fulfilment is so complex, however. A bit of work on your general relationship and lifestyle may be all that's needed to bring release to your passions.

Women are often more sensitive to the quality of their marriage than men. If you as a wife feel you and your husband aren't communicating properly, or have unresolved difficulties, you may well find you can't reach orgasm. Satisfaction comes easiest for you when you feel secure. You need to talk things out together, maybe with the help of trusted friends or counsellors, until you feel at peace.

Constant tiredness because of overwork and late nights can make you want to get sex over and done with. You rush your husband, make a few sympathetic responses then breathe a sigh of relief when he's done and fall gratefully asleep. But no orgasm. A review of your commitments and some early nights, or a few days' holiday, can make all the difference.

Tension and general anxiety will also temporarily hinder your enjoyment of love. You may be fearful about getting pregnant. Or afraid that you can be heard making love by the people in the flat down below, or the lodger, or the children. You'll have to talk this through with your husband and make what adjustments you can. Incidentally, we don't personally think it a good idea for newly-weds to take in lodgers unless it's absolutely unavoidable; they do put a strain on a young couple's relationship, however discreet you are.

Of course, your mood varies with the time of the month. There are days when you are very much 'the garden locked' and your husband will need a lot of skill with the keys if you are to reach orgasm. You'll find other occasions when you're feeling so randy that you'll throw wide the gates for him, as it were. Part of living together involves being sensitive to each other's moods and responding appropriately!

This brings us to the matter of experience and developing skill in the art of love-making. Mostly this involves patiently and thoroughly putting into practice the advice we've given in the previous chapters. Even if it takes a few weeks, in the majority of cases a wife will soon begin to experience orgasms on a regular basis. However, if any of the problems we've mentioned have been yours, or you're not finding things are succeeding, here are one or two additional ideas based upon a very successful Masters and Johnson therapy. Essentially they are ways of overcoming a wife's passivity by allowing her the freedom to set her own sexual pace with her husband instead of being hurtled along by his desires. You may find them helpful.

The first involves you and your husband sitting naked on the bed, you between his outspread legs and facing away from him with your own legs apart. You then take hold of his hands and use them to caress your own body where you want. He must let you take all the initiatives and you must be as uninhibited as you can. Direct his hands between your legs and rub your sexual organs with them in the way that gives you most pleasure. You can try to bring yourself to orgasm by this means. At the same time you should close your eyes and fill your mind with a good fantasy about your husband. This may be a romantic image or a blatantly sexual one. Or you can describe out loud what you're doing with his hands.

The second suggestion is that until the problem is solved you adopt the wife-on-top position for intercourse so that you make all the running.

You may then conclude intercourse with your husband more or less on his back and you lying almost on top with one of your legs straddling his. This allows your hips more freedom to respond to the contractions caused by orgasm.

Premature ejaculation

So far we've concentrated mostly upon the wife's problems, and those relating to lack of general love-making skills, but there's a fairly common difficulty in men known as premature ejaculation.

Some young husbands are so sexually keyed up that they cannot contain themselves long enough for their wives to reach orgasm. In acute cases a man may ejaculate as soon as he sees his wife's body or at the first touch. More likely, he may do so the moment he enters her vagina or within a very short time afterwards. Either way, it means disappointment for her and a sense of failure for him. Fortunately, it's not difficult to remedy this distressing state of affairs.

General muscular tension can cause premature ejaculation so it's important that you both relax before making love. You may wish to pray together first. Background music may help while you sip a quiet drink—hot chocolate or a small amount of alcohol if you imbibe (not too much or you'll get the opposite effect known descriptively as 'brewer's wilt'!).

Just occasionally previous rushed experiences outside of marriage, perhaps at parties or with prostitutes, may be an underlying anxiety trigger. These need bringing to the Lord for forgiveness so that a renewing of the mind can take place.

If your husband has a problem of not lasting more than a few seconds you can help him as his wife by using the following method.

With him lying on his back in a relaxed pose you rub the shaft of his penis, using your fingers, in an up-and-down motion until he tells you he's on the point of coming. You then stop and instead squeeze the head of his penis quite hard for three to four seconds, or you can give the head a sharp twist while holding it between your fingers and thumb. Another way is to squeeze the base of his penis with your finger lying across the underside just in front of his testicles. Any of these methods will immediately quench his desire to ejaculate. You should then recommence the original masturbatory motion until he again says he's nearly there. Stop and repeat the squeeze... and so on for fifteen to twenty minutes at a session.

After several of these sessions, you then adopt the woman-on-top position. As soon as he's ready to ejaculate you withdraw from him, give him the squeeze, and reinsert his penis into your vagina. You repeat this until you're so close to your own orgasm that you no longer care.

Using this technique will help him develop self-control after just a few sessions. It will also help if you make love frequently so that he's not at bursting point when you do come together. We hope you'll want to do that anyway!

From the husband's point of view, if your problem isn't too acute you can slow yourself down by using long, slow thrusts interspersed with pauses. We recommend that at first you learn to pause with your penis nearly withdrawn. Later on you can do it while fully inserted and substitute the rotatory motion on your wife's clitoris, which will delight her without pushing you too far.

You can also delay your climax by recognizing that much of sexual excitement is in the mind. So develop the knack of thinking about something decidedly unsexy whenever you feel yourself coming too quickly—dustbins, paying the bills, your socks—anything so long as it turns you off! It's all in a good cause.

Gradually you'll extend the time you can remain in your wife without ejaculating until you can more or less decide when you're going to climax and be able to guarantee her reaching orgasm. But even if at first you do find you're always getting there before her, all is not lost. Too many couples make the mistake of feeling everything is over once the husband has ejaculated, but that need not be the case. Rather than leaving her frustrated halfway up the hill, all you need do is carry on thrusting after you have ejaculated in order to take her over the top.

You have quite a few seconds before your penis shrinks, but even as it does you can still keep it well pressed into her and continue to rock your pelvic bone against her clitoris. Provided she doesn't lose heart she can reciprocate and will soon reach her orgasm. As an alternative, you can support your body rigidly on your toes and forearms so that you are resting lightly on her. She can then bring herself to orgasm by writhing against you. This all requires consideration on your part, but it's more than worth it just to see your wife's satisfaction. And, as an added bonus, at least in your earlier years, you'll find on occasions that you yourself stiffen up again for a second climax. That's not to be missed!

If you've used a condom you'll have to modify this approach because you must withdraw quickly to make the contraception effective. In this case you should massage your wife's clitoris with your hand in order to bring her to orgasm.

Mutual climax

The secret of pacing yourselves for simultaneous orgasm lies in gaining experience of putting into effect all our previous counsel about foreplay and actual intercourse. Again, we can't stress enough the importance of the wife being thoroughly prepared by her husband so that she's really ready to receive him. In fact, she should feel that if he carried on with the caresses she'd soon reach orgasm anyway. That's the fundamental key.

The second is to develop skill in varying the pace, pressure and style of intercourse. Although we've suggested the use of a stop-start method of control which is particularly suited to the inexperienced and short-fused husband, as you gain experience you'll want something more sophisticated.

In the early months of marriage you'll want to cultivate steady rock and roll rhythms of intercourse. (Yes, the musical term did originate from sexual associations!) With practice you'll develop several rhythms and be able to switch from one to the other at will. The simple secret is for the wife never to lie there passively but to always rock her hips in response to her husband's thrusts or to initiate the rhythm herself.

Reaching a mutual climax depends upon using this steady rhythm and accelerating either yourself or your partner so that you stay in tandem as much as possible.

A few sexual experiences will teach you when you need to speed up your wife. It's especially helpful if she tells you how she's doing—'I'm nearly there', 'Not yet', 'I've still a way to go', and so on. Extra pressure or rolling motions on her clitoris either with your pelvic bone or with your fingers will accelerate her. Try some long, slow strokes or twitch your penis in her. If she has sensitive breasts some extra fondling of her nipples using either your hand or your mouth will help. Kissing the side of her neck, chewing her earlobe or twirling your tongue in her ear may prove very exciting. Or how about some husky words of passionate endearment, an unashamedly earthy and erotic description of what her body is doing for you?

As the wife you can further stimulate yourself by caressing him with the palms of your hands or with your mouth. If you engage him in some prolonged mouth-to-mouth kissing it will stir you and be thoroughly enjoyable for him but will at the same time slow his movements. You can also try placing his hands on your breasts or buttocks and getting him to squeeze. Or you could change positions so that you're on top and he can have easy access to your clitoris without him speeding up.

Sometimes you'll get ahead of your man. You may have been feeling so aroused that you reach orgasm very quickly. To be honest there's not a lot of point in slowing you down! Your husband can either go full tilt and you'll make it together short, sharp and sweet; or he can let you get there, rest a few moments and then commence long, slow inter-course to bring you to orgasm again, only this time with him. If you do want to speed him up you can adapt the ideas we gave for him accelerating your passion.

However you do it, or however long you choose to take, there will come the point when neither of you wants to wait any longer and you'll go for the race down the home straight. This acceleration will normally be initiated by the husband. If he's learned self-control he can wait for the trigger of his wife gasping, 'I'm coming' or, 'I'm almost there.' The ideal is for the woman to arrive a fraction of a second before the man.

This is the moment to abandon all restraint and control. You should both throw everything you've got into this; hard, rapid thrusts from the husband, passionate writhings from the wife as she forces her vulva up against her man until both explode into ecstasy.

You can heighten the experience in a number of ways. Kissing deeply or thrusting your tongue into your partner's ear will do it, as will clutching hard or a stinging slap on the bottom, even digging your fingernails in or administering a love bite (preferably where it won't show!). We're not suggesting real harm, it's just that mild pain of this kind stimulates the same kind of nerves as those involved in orgasm and so adds to the brain's perception of the pleasure.

At a more subtle level we suggest that you consciously focus all your feelings of love onto your partner as you reach your climax. Will yourselves to merge together as one personality bathed in love. Pour out as much feeling of gratitude and appreciation as you can muster. And be full of thanksgiving to the Lord. You won't be the first to shout 'Hallelujah!' at such a moment! Sexual climax should be an act of worship.

*   *   *

Once a man has ejaculated he needs time before he can repeat the performance. This may be from only five to thirty minutes when he is young, to twenty-four hours or more in later years. The same isn't true for a woman. Your wife is capable of having more than one orgasm at a time.

Now we've come across books which make a woman sound frigid if she doesn't have half a dozen orgasms at a time and several love-making sessions a day into the bargain. So we'd just like to dispel some illusions about this. For a man it's the violent spurting of semen for a few seconds coupled with the inner sexual release which satisfies him. Many women respond in a similar way and have one giant explosive orgasm which blows their mind and leaves them physically shattered. Others may have an ascending (or descending) series of smaller ones. Sometimes a wife's orgasm will last a few seconds, other times it will go on for more than a minute until she almost begs for mercy. Occasionally it will be no more than a satisfying rise of feeling which then gently dies away. There will be times when the experience is absolutely earth-shattering in its intensity. It all depends. You mustn't get under a bondage of false expectation. Everyone is different, and provided *you* feel satisfied, that's all that matters.

We suggest that as the husband you let your wife decide whether she wants more than one orgasm. This is simply done: once you've ejaculated you continue the motions of intercourse for as long as her climax lasts, and beyond, so that she can climb to another orgasm...and another...and another if she wishes. When she cries, 'No more!' you stop, whether that's after one or several orgasms. As we've already indicated, if you've used a sheath for contraception you'll have to do this by hand. This will also be the best policy if you find your penis tends to get sore due to prolonged intercourse following your climax.

When all's said and done there will be occasions when she doesn't make it. If you've had a good time of love play that won't be disastrous for her. There's always tomorrow. But what we don't want you to do is settle for a mentality which says, 'It's the game not the scoring that matters.' Normally, your wife should expect to reach orgasm with you. Not to score a goal in the odd match is all right, but if you never score you might just feel like giving up the game, and that will never do.

One last matter concerns the afterglow to intercourse. This is a time of happy repose, of deep satisfaction and thanksgiving. It's important that you express this to each other. A husband needs to remember that although his passion subsides rapidly his wife comes down more gradually —do you recall the graph earlier? She needs further caresses, kisses and words of love to make her satisfaction complete— the chocolate mints after the meal, if you like. And both of you will appreciate being told how superb you were. Generous praise is rare in our cynical society, but it's one of the best investments any of us can make in our partner in love. This is a good moment to give thanks to the Lord also.

There's no particular need to wash after intercourse. In fact, vaginal douches upset the natural chemical balance of the vagina. Sperm isn't dirty, in any case. If you find the mixture of your own juices and your husband's sperm running out a problem then a tissue between your legs will blot it up.

Making love is the finest relaxant we know and you should fall into peaceful slumber afterwards. If you're making love earlier in the day you'll probably have to get up, but don't rush unless it's unavoidable. A time of relaxation is part of the joy and renewal of love. Anyway, you might just want to do it again if you lie there.

Or maybe you'd like to try something extra special....

12

Let's Celebrate!

Real life bears little resemblance to the romantic situations portrayed in love stories and television beauty-aid commercials. It's not a horse-drawn carriage emerging from the morning mist that greets you, but the washing up, the ironing and the shopping list. That power boat slicing through a racing tide to rescue a damsel in distress is more likely to be you stuck in a traffic jam and late home for tea once again. And when the sinking sun sizzles into the Aegean, that toga-clad Adonis and Venus sipping nectar is you and the missus slumped in front of the telly with a cup of instant coffee each, wondering if you've the energy to visit Auntie Flo or not—let alone make mad, passionate love before sleep claims you for the night!

However skilled you become at making love the reality of workaday life means that you're going to do it mostly late at night, tired and without any special effects. That doesn't mean it'll be mediocre, let's hasten to add. If you follow our advice then love-making will still be the high point of even your most routine days. Like a good daily meal it will contain sufficient variety and content to leave you thoroughly satisfied. Everyday sex doesn't have to be merely bread-and-butter sex.

But there is more. There's a place for what we're calling celebration sex—a slap-up feed, a bit of a party, something out of the ordinary, even *risqué* if you like.

Sexual celebrations are like spices. They add piquancy to the feast of love and keep the palate from becoming jaded. They are also fun, not to say a little silly, and that's good for us. It never does to take ourselves too seriously—especially as far as our sexual prowess is concerned. Who can't but be amused when such a noble virtue as love has to be expressed through these panting, squelchy bodies of ours? Ridiculous we are, and it befits us to join in the laughter on occasions.

What we've done is to group a few celebration ideas under four themes gleaned from the Song of Songs. We've tried to be realistic and avoid the utterly impractical. A few years ago women all over the country were reacting to the suggestion that they should greet their husbands on the doorstep wearing little other than boots and bangles. Everyone knew you were bound to open the door to a double-glazing salesman or a Jehovah's Witness! We've kept that in mind. You may still think some of our ideas are crazy. Provided you're not just being strait-laced that doesn't matter. What we really hope is that we'll spark off some ideas in your own imagination so that you develop your own repertoire of celebration specials.

So here's a few thoughts to get you going.

The garden

'....our bed is verdant [shaded with branches—New English Bible]. The beams of our house are cedars; our rafters are firs' (Song of Songs 1:16–17).

Yes, this couple were making love out of doors! And what better place in a warm climate? Provided you can find a truly secluded spot, of course. Having intercourse in the open air isn't as easy as it was in Solomon's day; there are more people about—and we do have laws against indecent exposure. But that's not to say you can't find deserted spots....

The garden theme really means making love somewhere other than the bedroom. You may possibly possess the right kind of garden or have access to a remote beach or heath for a session under the stars. You could always take a small tent with you, of course—and at least a blanket! Or if courage and opportunity fail you, modern cars do have reclining seats.

You may not get as far as the great outdoors, but do at least make it to the sofa. What better way to spend an evening than to make love before an open fire (if you've got one), with low lights, soft music and a bottle of wine? Or you may like to start under the shower or in the bath and see where you finish up. Not drowned, we hope! Then there's the dining room table, the kitchen floor, the attic, the stairs—and when you've tried all these you can do something really kinky and use the bed!

Another time, another place. The garden theme is a simple way of bringing some extra tang into your love-life.

The dance

'.... come back, that we may gaze on you!

Why would you gaze on the Shulammite as on the dance of Mahanaim?

How beautiful your sandalled feet, O prince's daughter!' (Song of Songs 6:13–7:1).

The young bride dances to display her charms. She is either naked or, more likely, scantily clad. Her lover is entranced and pours forth a tribute to her beauty.

Whether you think so or not, your husband finds your body beautiful and you can bring great delight to your love-life by using it to seduce him visually. A few alluring garments can be useful. Fortunately, quite sexy underwear and so forth is readily available from chain stores and regular mail order catalogues nowadays. Find out what your husband likes and what displays you to your best advantage. You may not have a fashion model figure, or even think some clothes are much of a turn on, but it's the effect on your man that you're going for, and that's what matters most.

Incidentally, as we mentioned in chapter 9, a preference for particular garments isn't in itself kinky. It's only if items of clothing become *necessary* for sexual arousal, or the object of desire in themselves, that the person has become a fetishist.[1] What we're talking about is a bit of fun, a love game.

If you're an outgoing woman you might like to emulate the Shulammite and dance before your husband. Or you could try putting on a one-girl striptease show for him. As an alternative, how about serving his evening meal topless or wearing just a frilly white apron? Careful he doesn't get indigestion!

To be a bit more sophisticated you could send him out for half an hour with the promise of 'something special' upon his return. When he comes back he'll find you bathed, perfumed and lounging scantily clad on the sofa in some frilly bit of nonsense.

More subtle variations of the dance-display theme are simply letting him know or discover that you've left your bra off or forgotten to put your panties on when you go out for the evening—this one for warm months only! You can get his imagination running riot with little ideas like this so that he's raring to go by the time you get home. Really, the possibilities are endless.

The tryst

'I will get up now and go about the city, through its streets and squares; I will search for the one my heart loves' (Song of Songs 3:2).

Do you recall the joy of meeting each other somewhere during your courtship? You observe it now in others. The girl standing on the street corner waiting expectantly for her boyfriend, eyes glancing this way and that until she sees him. He, hastening along the street, eager not to keep her waiting. Their eyes light up as they spot each other. She smiles as he runs towards her. They kiss. The lovers' tryst.

You don't have to lose that sense of lovers meeting once

---

[1] Transvestism, dressing in the clothes of the opposite sex, is condemned in Deuteronomy 22:5. This probably refers to both blatant trans-sexual display and deliberate deception. Obsessive transvestism is indicative of a sexual identity crisis and requires specialist counsel.

you're married. The tryst provides an opportunity to retain a youthful romance in your relationship. As an example, why not try meeting somewhere after work? Play the romantic lover and give her red roses, take her to a restaurant for a candlelit meal, have a stroll by the river, then return home to consummate your love in a passionate session on the sofa.

If you fancy developing this love game a bit more you could arrange to travel by different routes to a common rendezvous, say a theatre, pub or restaurant. You could pretend you've met for the first time and act out a whirlwind romance, getting 'married' on the way home before reliving your honeymoon night.

Seek-and-find games of this kind remind you that the flame hasn't died. If you could start all over again you'd still choose each other and fall madly in love. That can give quite a fillip to your love-making.

The retreat

'Come, my lover, let us go to the countryside, let us spend the night in the villages' (Song of Songs 7:11).

Here's a pleasant invitation, a romantic night away in the countryside. In the case of this pair of lovers, doing it under the stars again!

You could book into a small hotel or an inn for a night or two. Some of our most precious times of love have been when we've escaped from the hassle of everyday life just to be alone together. It does wonders for our relationship and we thoroughly recommend it. A change of environment, no chores and no interruptions, can release a whole new dimension of leisurely love-making; a second honeymoon, only this time with experience!

A really nice way of doing this is to spring it as a surprise on your partner. Make all the arrangements, including someone to have the children if you've got any. Ensure the diary is kept clear. Then whisk her away for an exciting weekend or even mid-week break. You'll be amazed at what it will do for the quality of your marriage, especially if you've both been very busy of late.

These then are some celebratory ideas. You can, of course, weave all four themes together and embroider them with some creative love-making techniques until you've a considerable tapestry of memorable experiences to look back on and many more to come. Naturally, some ideas are more practicable at different times of life. It's easier before children come along and after they've grown up. But there are still plenty of exciting possibilities, even when the odds seem stacked against anything other than a routine life. All it takes is a little imagination, a bit of effort and faith that God wants to bless you abundantly out of his generous heart of love.

The art of love-making is a skill acquired by practice. Provided you know how to go about it—and we've hopefully set you on the right lines—with patience and consideration you'll create your very own joint masterpiece. Nobody else will see it but they'll recognise its fruit in two happy, secure and loving people who know they've really got it together.

And that's a constant cause for celebration.

HAVING CHILDREN

It's beyond the scope of this book to cover all that's involved in raising a family. However, we felt it important to include some advice about conceiving a baby and about sex during and after pregnancy.

We've also included a chapter on the relationship between your love-life and the sex education of your children as they grow up.

13

Starting a Family

Like most couples, sooner or later you'll probably want to have children.

There's no more wonderful gift given to us by God than the ability to reproduce after our kind. What parents fail to be fascinated by the birth of their own child, conceived as the fruit of their love?

'He's got your eyes!'

'Hm, but that's definitely your nose.'

'Look at those tiny fingers.'

'Marvellous, isn't it? And all our own work.'

'Mm, but with a little help from you know who.'

Actually, with quite a lot of help from 'you know who'! When God said to Adam and Eve at the dawn of history, 'Be fruitful and multiply, and fill the earth' (Genesis 1:28, rsv), he didn't simply delegate the responsibility to them and then withdraw into deep space. Instead he graciously permitted them to become partners with him in the task of creating new life. When you start a family you're not only doing something godlike but you get involved with God himself.

The partnership isn't always recognized, especially in a technological world of contraceptives, test-tube babies, artificial insemination and cloning experiments, where the marriage bed seems in danger of giving way to the chemistry set. Yet God is still the author of life; we are his offspring and in him we all live and move and have our being (Acts 17:28). The psalmist rightly sings, 'For you created my inmost being; you knit me together in my mother's womb...your eyes saw my unformed body [literally embryo]' (Psalm 139:13, 16). The timeless story of Ruth expresses it perfectly. 'So Boaz took Ruth and she became his wife; and he went in to her, and the Lord gave her conception, and she bore a son' (Ruth 4:13, RSV).

This means, for Christians at least, that starting a family is a spiritual issue. What is the will of God? This is more important when it comes to making a decision than whether you've got enough money or have done all the travelling you want, let alone whether you've purchased the ideal property and landed in a secure job. These factors need taking into consideration, but they ought not to be the determining ones.

In general terms we can say it is the will of God for a couple to have children. The deliberately childless marriage has not only a certain selfishness about it but lacks a central part of God's purpose for marriage itself. 'Has not the Lord made them one? In flesh and spirit they are his. And why one? Because he was seeking godly offspring' (Malachi 2:15). There's no finer or more far-reaching ministry we can perform than to raise children who grow up to love and serve the Lord.

We should add that it's generally the will of God that we start our families while we're young. Child-bearing is certainly best suited to women in their prime of life, and raising them needs parents with an awful lot of energy and adaptability. There are exceptions to this, of course, and in any case babies are likely to come over a number of years.

How many children you should have is a matter to be decided before God. Psalm 127:5 says, 'Blessed is the man whose quiver is full of them.' You need to know when you've reached that point—quivers vary in size quite considerably!

So, from the very commencement of your marriage you'll want to have this subject in your prayers. Of course, the Lord may just pre-empt all your plans by letting you get pregnant through failed contraceptives. As we said earlier, many 'accidents' turn out to be the will of God! If it happens this way for you, then do receive the new life as a gift from him. He's Lord of all circumstances and he who gave the child will also provide the means for you to raise that child. We feel strongly that the wilful sacrificing of children's lives by abortion to suit our conveniences has no place in a Christian marriage. Love your baby!

Faith and works go hand in hand. When, in the normal course of events, the Lord gives you the go-ahead to start a family, you have to act upon it intelligently. For example, the couple who have intercourse infrequently, and then always at the wrong time of the month, are unlikely ever to start a family. We'd like to offer some practical suggestions to assist getting pregnant.

We mentioned earlier that if you've been using the pill you should change to another form of contraceptive, for example the condom, some three months before you try for a baby. This is to allow time for your hormones and reproductive system to settle back into a natural routine. Similarly, if you use an IUD we recommend you use another contraceptive until you've had at least one clear period in order to let your womb restabilize.

Most people don't, in fact, want to choose the sex of their children, but all sorts of ideas abound for trying to influence the course of nature. They range from old wives tales about which side you should lie on after intercourse, through special acidity-modifying diets, to artificial insemination by sperm taken from the bottom of a test-tube where the males are said to congregate. If it's true that God creates our inmost being, knows us even before we're conceived and has a unique destiny for each of us to fulfil, then presumably he also determines our sex. We preferred at least to give him the option rather than trying to take the matter into our own hands. We suspect most Christians feel the same.

The majority of women get pregnant very quickly without any fuss or difficulty at all, but it's estimated that some 10%

of married couples cannot have any children and another 15% have fewer than they would like because of difficulties in conceiving. The reasons for this are many and varied. Some problems are easily solved, others require nothing short of a miracle—but miracles do occur.

We're going to run through some of the exacting conditions necessary to reproduction, pointing out some of the things that can go wrong and suggesting easy remedies wherever possible. If nonetheless you have no success after two years of trying, you should seek medical advice in order to ascertain the cause of the problem.

Ovulation

In order to conceive a woman must ovulate. A baby girl starts life with between 400,000 and one million unripe ova in sacs called follicles. From the time she reaches puberty through to the menopause one of these will ripen each month and detach itself from an ovary to be picked up by the tentacled end of a Fallopian tube where it will be carried to await possible fertilization. If that occurs the fertilized egg will pass into the womb where it will attach itself and grow into a fully-fledged baby. If it isn't fertilized it will simply pass out in the normal secretions. That's assuming all goes well.

Things can go wrong. Ovarian cysts may prevent ova from ripening. Fibroids (non-cancerous growths) can block the Fallopian tubes or prevent the egg attaching itself to the uterus. Other diseases can cause damage or inflammation of the tubes so preventing a clear passage for the egg. IUDs sometimes cause infections which do this. Surgical damage to the womb or cervix resulting from an abortion may prevent the egg implanting. Genetic malfunction may cause the egg to spontaneously abort. Changes in the vaginal acidity may mean sperm cannot survive even to reach the egg.

Fortunately, these conditions are not too common and no woman should suspect anything just because she doesn't get pregnant immediately.

Emotional stress can often prevent a woman from conceiving either by messing up her hormonal cycle or by putting her Fallopian tubes into a spasm so that the egg can't pass through. It may be rooted in anxiety or fear, or unresolved conflict with her husband. This can lead to a vicious circle as a failure to conceive for months on end can in itself generate tension. Should you find yourself in this unfortunate situation we recommend that you stop 'trying' to have a baby and instead just relax and enjoy your love-making. Many a couple finds that taking a holiday and talking out the problems soon leads to pregnancy. If necessary you should seek some outside counsel together as well.

Understandably, general ill health, exhaustion and poor diet may reduce your hormones to below the level necessary for ovulation. You may also develop irregular periods. Strangely enough, overfitness can have the same effect. Superfit women often cease to have periods and research indicates that this is related to the percentage of body fat they carry. If that falls to below 16–18% the hormonal mechanisms won't be triggered. The average young woman carries 26% fat compared to a man's 12%. This difference approximates to 300,000 kJ—more or less the energy required to produce a full-term baby.[1]

More rest, improved diet and less hyperactivity fortunately remedies the situation very quickly. It's all a matter of healthy balance really.

Sperm production

A man must generate sufficient live and healthy sperm, as well as enough seminal fluid to protect them against vaginal acidity. General debility, overwork, obesity and lack of exercise will hinder sperm production. It may be a sad commentary upon our Western lifestyle that the average sperm count

[1] Craig Sharp, 'Physiology and the woman athlete' (*New Scientist*, 2nd August 1984).
Jim Fixx, 'Women on the move' (*Running Magazine*, September 1985).

of the American male has fallen by 30% over the past fifty years. Diseases such as mumps in adulthood can produce sterility (though not a loss of virility, so your love-life won't be affected) as can exposure to toxic chemicals or radiation.

At a more commonplace level it's worth remembering that sperm cannot survive extremes of cold and heat. The man who has a hot bath prior to making love to his wife may well have killed off most of his sperm for the evening. Overtight underpants can have the same effect, especially if you work in a warm environment. The testicles are in a sac outside the body because sperm need to be kept at a lower temperature.

Prolonged abstinence from intercouse will cause a decline in sperm production, but if a man makes love too frequently he may not be giving his sperm time to mature. Abstaining for a day or so before your wife ovulates (see below) will be sufficient if you think this may be a problem.

Timing

Assuming both of you are functioning correctly, to start a baby you must have intercourse. That may sound ridiculously obvious but it's a fact that many aspiring parents just don't do it often enough or at the right time for conception to occur.

You have only a few days during each periodic cycle when you can hope to begin a new life. Those days are determined by the life span of sperm in the womb—about two to three days—and by the viability of the ovum—around twenty-four hours. In all, there are five to six days a month when conception is possible. Have another look at the rhythm method chart in chapter 4. This time you're deliberately aiming to have intercourse on the *unsafe* days.

If you are a woman with a regular twenty-eight-day cycle, making love during each of the eleventh to sixteenth days, counting from day one of your period, is most likely to get you pregnant. Should you have irregular cycles varying between twenty-seven to thirty-five days, conception is most probable if you have intercourse on alternate days beginning with the thirteenth and ending with the twenty-first, again counting from the first day of your period.

It also helps to use positions of deep penetration and to rest for a while afterwards. You may like to draw your knees up to your chin and clasp them while lying on your back for ten to fifteen minutes. This allows gravity to assist the sperm in entering the neck of your womb. You can, of course, have intercourse in this position.

Some women have a retroverted womb, that is, it tilts the wrong way. This is quite harmless, but you may find that the rear-entry position, illustrated in chapter 10, aids conception if you have this condition. You should, in any case, adopt this posture after intercourse for a while if you wish to help the sperm into the neck of your womb.

There are a number of treatments available to help infertile couples. We just want to stress the importance and effectiveness of prayer. There are many modern testimonies of the Lord granting children to previously sterile couples and we recommend you seek him, especially before contemplating fertility drugs, laboratory fertilization or artificial insemination. Space unfortunately doesn't permit us to discuss the moral implications of these techniques. But this one we can commend:

> Isaac prayed to the Lord on behalf of his wife, because she was barren. The Lord answered his prayer, and his wife Rebekah became pregnant (Genesis 25:21).

*   *   *

All being well you'll shortly find you've missed a period. That may be coupled with morning sickness, sore breasts, tingly nipples and feeling emotionally very vulnerable—though many women experience none of these symptoms. The way to find out for certain if you're pregnant is to buy a home-test kit from your chemist and check a urine sample—or wait until you start bulging!

Babies in the womb are people. Many fascinating observations have been made about their ability to respond to outside stimuli. This shouldn't surprise us. Long ago John the Baptist leapt for joy in his mother's womb at the greeting of Mary, herself pregnant with Jesus (Luke 1:41–44). Your baby is already about two weeks old when you notice you've missed your period and may be nearly a month old before the pregnancy is finally confirmed. He's fully formed and has a personality of his own by the time you get the first butterfly movements in your tummy. We've been told that the Chinese celebrate a child's first birthday just three months after he's born—which makes sense when you think about it. So we'd encourage you to start praying and caring for your child as soon as you become aware of his existence. There's no need to be overprotective of yourself physically—just use common-sense—but do keep spiritually and emotionally in harmony with God. Not a bad thing to do in any case!

An average pregnancy lasts 266 days, though depending upon your menstrual cycle, general health and hereditary factors, yours may last up to eight to ten days longer. You may, of course, give birth prematurely.

To calculate the approximate date of your confinement you count three months back from the start of your last period and add seven days. For example, last period started: 10th May. Count back three months: 10th April, 10th March, 10th February. Add seven days: 17th February. Nine times out of ten the ante-natal clinic will tell you you've got your dates hopelessly wrong because your baby is too big/too small/twins/triplets/you should have been induced last week/ are you sure you're pregnant? You'll just have to live with all that and comfort yourself in the knowledge that you're not producing a British Standard Baby! But do check your dates, though.

Pregnancy isn't an illness and although we believe in general that it's right to attend the ante-natal clinic, particularly for your first baby, you must be careful not to let the medical experts have too much of a place in your mind. The fact that things *can* go wrong doesn't mean they are necessarily going to. A lot of mums-to-be suffer needless anxieties and submit to more tests and investigations than are needed, some of which actually increase the risk of damage, simply because the hospital is playing ultra-safe or a student is doing a project, or even because of the fear of litigation if a baby is born deformed. We suggest you opt for a minimum, insist on knowing what every test is for,[2] and take advice from other sensible couples who've been through it all.

There's no reason to stop having sexual intercourse during pregnancy, unless you start losing blood. In that case you should take to your bed, call your minister in to pray and seek medical advice if necessary. But in the normal course of events love-making does no harm to the mother or the baby. You may find, as do many women, that you are in the peak of health during the midpart of your pregnancy and more easily sexually aroused than usual. This is a good thing for your husband too, because he isn't carrying the baby and his sexual needs remain the same as ever. Even if normal intercourse does become impractical for any reason, you should still offer to relieve him by hand.

Making love during pregnancy is a positive contribution to your mutual well-being and, therefore, good for your child. And many a joke may be had about your baby's response to this strange object which nightly thrusts its way in! Not that a penis or sperm come anywhere near, of course. The neck of the womb is positively sealed against any such intrusion.

As the pregnancy proceeds some methods of intercourse will become difficult because of the growing size of your wife's tummy. You may well find it helpful to adopt one of the rear-entry positions or try the one where she lies on her back with her bottom on the edge of the bed so that you can enter

[2] For example, a doctor should not perform the test for spina bifida (AFP test) without discussing it with you. If it is positive, you are confronted with either choosing an abortion or *knowing* you are going to carry a deformed child to full term. This can be very traumatic, especially if you find abortion morally unacceptable.

from an upright, kneeling position. Your aim is to keep your weight off her abdomen.

Many couples succeed in having intercourse all the way through to the ninth month (and beyond!) with just a little bit of adjustment. This can easily be one of the most beautiful periods of loving intimacy in your life together, as the wonderful relationship between love-making and life-giving dawns upon you.

*   *   *

Once your baby is born, life is changed for ever. The first thing you notice is that he or she demands your full attention. Infants require feeding, changing, cuddling and winding several times a day—and night. You quickly realize that you are no longer just two people; from now on all your routines and plans will have to take account of your child.

This can make life a bit difficult during those first few weeks after the birth, what with the new responsibilities, the tiredness and the readjustments. A combination of these factors together with hormonal imbalances can send some women into post-natal depression. With prayer and patience this will pass, but it's a very real trial for those who go through it.

On top of this a mother may be suffering discomfort down below because of stitches required to mend a tear or surgical incision. She may develop sore breasts and nipples because of feeding. So a husband needs to be very supportive and sympathetic at this time.

If all is well you can recommence intercourse as little as two weeks after the delivery, but if there are any complications you may have to wait six or eight weeks. This can seem a very long time, especially if intercourse wasn't possible towards the end of the pregnancy. Some men find themselves resenting the baby because of its intrusion into the marriage, taking up all the wife's attention and causing prolonged sexual abstinence.

It will help if you speak honestly to one another about these things. As a wife you can relieve your husband by hand and once the soreness of delivery is past he can bring you to orgasm by the same means. If you both kiss and cuddle a lot you'll find you'll cope with this short phase of life and lose none of the joy which a new-born baby will bring to you.

Once you do resume normal sexual relations you'll need to start using contraceptives straightaway, unless you want another baby in nine months' time. Breast-feeding doesn't guarantee you won't get pregnant.

One of the first things you'll notice about your wife is that she feels different. Her vagina is no longer a tight fit and the angles don't seem the same. Her breasts are larger and she may still be carrying some excess weight from the pregnancy. You may be just a little disappointed with intercourse, especially if she isn't able to rise to orgasm on the first few occasions. This could be because it's a bit painful and you should, therefore, go gently. In spite of the changes she's still the woman you love and things will soon settle back to normal again.

To assist this process it's ever so important that you do your post-natal exercises diligently. Many women don't, to their later cost. By neglecting them, muscles and tissues can be permanently impaired. This can not only affect your love-making and future pregnancies, but may leave you liable to a prolapsed womb or poor bladder control in later life.

Particularly important are the pelvic-floor exercises. These aim to strengthen the tissues which hold everything in place underneath. They also tighten the muscles surrounding your vagina so that your husband's penis fits snugly once more. They are sometimes called PC (short for the unpronounceable *pubococcygeus*) exercises.

You can do the most important one anywhere—sitting, lying or standing, with your legs slightly apart. You may have to concentrate a bit at first to get it right and it can help if you try it once or twice while sitting on the loo with your knees wide apart.

First you tighten the muscle controlling your anus, then do the same with the one around your vagina and finally pull up your insides as though you were trying not to pass water. With all these muscles clenched you count to four. Then relax. Repeat the exercise ten times and do several sessions a day (or twenty contractions every time you do the washing up), for at least three months and as often as you can throughout life. If you're doing it correctly you should soon be able to insert a finger into your vagina and grip it quite tightly by contracting the muscles. Your husband will certainly notice the difference.

We can't stress enough the value of getting yourself fit again after childbirth. With just a bit of effort you can lose the weight, regain the muscle tone and look as though you've never had a baby. This is important for your sense of self-esteem. Many a wife feels she's gone to pot in the course of her pregnancy. The sheer demand of a new baby can make her feel she's no more than a bloated milking and nappy-changing machine, however much she's in other ways fulfilled. It doesn't have to be like that.

As a husband you can encourage your wife; boost her self-confidence with loving words, share the practical responsibilities of caring for the baby so that she's got time to think of herself, and buy her some new clothes as soon as she begins to get her figure back. Let her know just how much you esteem her and she'll never lack a sense of her own self-worth.

Babies change your life, they don't ruin it. As you share the joys and responsibilities you'll enter a new depth of love and commitment to each other. Not least, that will be expressed in a more profound sexual satisfaction than you've ever known before. In turn, that will bless your growing family.

But more of that in the next chapter.

14

Sex Education

From the moment children arrive on the scene your sex life ceases to be a wholly private affair. As with every other aspect of your relationship it becomes the subject of their insatiable curiosity. In all innocence they poke the bits that no one except your partner is allowed to touch; they quite properly enjoy a level of physical intimacy forbidden to the outside world. And they ask the most shocking questions, usually at the least opportune moment.

Every mum gets it sooner or later, as likely as not at the supermarket checkout or when sipping tea with her mother-in-law.

'Mummy, where do babies come from?'

This is followed by, 'Well, who plants the seed?'

Which leads quite naturally to the sixty-four thousand dollar question, 'How does Daddy plant the seed?'

You're faced with a crucial choice at this point, as is Dad when he staggers in from work to be confronted by his child's innocent question: 'Are you going to plant any seeds in Mummy tonight, Daddy?' Do you tell the truth, concoct a fairy story or make it clear this is not a polite subject to talk about?

Honest answers

Many parents still take the last course because sex is associated with shame, guilt and secrecy in their own minds. Children don't think like this in their infancy; they accept nudity, feeling their genitals and questions about where babies come from as part of the commonplace of life. It's those parents who project their own hang-ups onto their children who turn sex into a taboo subject for them.

It doesn't take long for children to realize that the topic causes embarrassment to their parents. So they stop asking questions and become secretive about it. They pick up the street lore from other children. The often inadequate and morally confused sex education they get at school has to suffice, and they won't let their parents see the homework. In the end they may finish up in immorality as a reaction against their parents' prudishness.

If you want your children to keep sex within the sanctity of marriage the least you must do is to be open about the subject within the family circle. To our minds that means answering their questions honestly as they arise. Rather than ducking the issues with outmoded tales about storks and gooseberry bushes it's better to tell them the plain, unvarnished truth. Half the time you'll bore them stiff because, of course, they won't understand it all, but at least they'll know that it's a subject they can talk about—even if at times you do wish they would wait until there are no eavesdroppers around!

As your children grow up you'll be able to gear your answers to their own development so that, rather than having one embarrassing puberty-onset talk about the birds and the bees, you'll have taught them all they need to know along the way. It's then quite easy to chat through specifically the changes which accompany adolescence, such as menstruation, nocturnal emissions, physical development and emotional ups and downs.

This approach will create an openness in your relationship which will be of great value during the teenage years. If you can talk about sex, you can talk about anything! And teen-agers do need to be able to talk to their parents. Today they're confronted with conflicting moralities. They have to think through homosexual options. Do I go on the pill like everyone else in my class? What's wrong with sleeping with your girlfriend/boyfriend if you're in love? Wouldn't it be better not to marry but just live together—and there are tax advantages, aren't there?

They like you to notice that they're developing. Girls want you to keep measuring their busts, boys want you to feel their biceps. They almost count the number of hairs they've grown. Above all, they want to know that they're normal. Being able to share at this level with Mum and Dad is the best gift a teenager can have.

This sort of frankness doesn't develop overnight; it has to be there from the beginning so that there's a good foundation to carry you through the tempestuous teenage years. We've noticed in our own experience that God gave us a kind of trial run for those teenage years during the first few years of our children's lives. What we sowed then in terms of honesty, love, discipline and friendship has borne fruit later on. In the words of Scripture, 'Train a child in the way he should go, and when he is old he will not turn from it' (Proverbs 22:6).

Masturbation

This is an issue which vexes many Christians. The secular answer is simple: regular masturbation is not only harmless but actually beneficial in providing healthy sexual release and experience of orgasm. The only thing wrong is feeling guilty about it. As to the origin of that guilt, it may be traced back to repressive parents who scolded or spanked their children when they caught them 'playing with themselves'. This attitude was fostered by the threat from the church of hell-fire for all such sins of lust. Now that we've proved no such threat exists we are free to indulge in this natural and universal pleasure to our heart's content.

This secular view is based upon the belief that you should enjoy whatever you like provided it doesn't harm you or others. There is no God nor any such thing as sin. Conscience is only put there by parents, and often wrongly.

Christians on the other hand believe that the living God has the right to demand a standard of behaviour from those made in his image. That includes exercising self-control over our sensual desires, not treating members of the opposite sex as objects of lust, and recognizing that the only proper use of our sexual gifts is as a shared expression of love within the marriage covenant.

The Bible nowhere condemns masturbation as such and we must, therefore, be careful not to be absolute where the Scriptures aren't. But at the same time we mustn't be afraid to apply biblical principles to present-day issues. As far as we can see, there are at least two things wrong with masturbation as it's usually practised: it's using a gift made for sharing in a self-indulgent manner, and it's more often than not accompanied by lustful fantasies. This twin abuse of God's purpose is what causes the guilt.

Jesus doesn't say, 'It's not real sin so ignore those feelings, break through the guilt barrier.' Instead he says,

> If your right eye causes you to sin, gouge it out and throw it away.... And if your right hand causes you to sin, cut it off and throw it away. It is better for you to lose one part of your body than for your whole body to go into hell (Matthew 5:29–30).

Does masturbating cause a person to lust in their thoughts? Does it replace self-control with self-indulgence? Does it tend to introvert a person's sexual desires? Does it become a habit, a kind of self-comfort apart from God? If so, Jesus would say deal drastically with it, not by literally severing your hand but by using it to serve God instead. Paul wrote,

> Do not offer the parts of your body to sin, as instruments of wickedness, but rather offer yourselves to God, as those who have been brought from death to life; and offer the parts of

your body to him as instruments of righteousness (Romans 6:13).

How then should we raise and counsel our children in this? When they're very young and fiddling with themselves while, say, having a nappy changed or on the potty, we suggest you completely ignore it. In all likelihood, curiosity satisfied, they'll just stop doing it. It's quite appropriate, of course, to discourage them from holding their genitals in public once they get a little older. Distracting them into doing something else is the best way.

If you do find your child has an excessive interest in his or her genitals beyond the age of about seven years, and you may either observe this or note some soreness, we recommend you have a low-key chat about it. Possibly the child is going through an insecure patch and looking for some kind of comfort. You need to find out, for example, whether difficulty at school (the work, a sarcastic teacher or being bullied) is at the root of it, and deal with that. If your child is just finding masturbation pleasurable we think it best if you tell them you agree that it is, but say it's a pleasure to be saved until they're married and can share it with their partner.

Because children are likely to be taught about masturbation in an unhelpful way at school you'll need to discuss it with them when they reach puberty. We suggest you teach them God's purpose for sex and positively encourage them to live an outgoing, active and purposeful teenage life. Explain too that young men sometimes have 'wet dreams' and that this is God's natural safety valve to cope with the production of sperm.

Almost everyone masturbates at some time or other. Although we feel it does normally involve sin, it isn't unforgiveable or even anything like the most serious. Children need to know that the Lord freely forgives all confessed sin, including those associated with masturbation.

Habitual masturbation is far more likely to become a problem for the introverted, insecure child. Without wishing to minimize the plain temptations to lust in our society, let alone the reality of growing sexual awareness, nonetheless a happy, positive teenager is likely to handle the pressures much more easily. And that's where parental attention needs to be focused.

Nudity

What about nudity in the family? Should children see their parents naked? It's not an issue spoken about clearly in the Scriptures. (The reference in Leviticus 18 to not uncovering the nakedness of near relatives is correctly translated in the New International Version to mean not having sexual intercourse with them. It is not a ban on nudity as such.)

Society is of little help here. We have certain conventions about clothing based upon a mixture of appropriateness, modesty and seduction. So we allow virtual nudity for the purpose of sunbathing but insist on formal attire for the office, for example. This isn't the place to discuss society's attitudes towards nudity except to say that quite properly you should teach your children to observe the accepted social proprieties in so far as they reflect biblical principles.

This means that you have to exercise your own wisdom within the family unit. Those who incline to an openness maintain that if children have seen it all they're spared the temptations for a naughty peek which come to children for whom nudity has been taboo. It also helps them to accept their own bodies as natural and good—which they are, of course.

If you decide to take this line you'll have to teach your children to act with discretion, especially when you have visitors. We also believe it's not right for children to see you having intercourse or engaging in heavy petting. Young children get very disturbed by this as they interpret the passionate movements as a violent fight between the pair of you! So you need a lock on the bedroom door or at least a verbal one which forbids them entry when you say so.

That doesn't mean they shouldn't see you kissing and cuddling. Nor need it be any secret to your teenage children that you still make love together, and passionately at that. Actually, it's a fact difficult to hide in the average semi-detached. Many a joke may be shared about the creaky bed which kept them awake the previous night!

Once your children reach puberty you'll have to reconsider continuing with household nudity. Children themselves go through a self-conscious phase at this time and you may just let the practice naturally drop. It's as well to mention that some fathers may find the presence of their naked, well-developed daughter a problem and some mothers can feel quite depressed by the comparison of their own figure with that of their child's. This whole matter is one which you should discuss together and come to a place of peace about before God.

A fear of incest shouldn't stop you hugging your teenage children. On the contrary they need to feel your physical affection more than ever. Many a person gets involved in pre-marital sex simply because of the desire to be hugged and accepted. Lots of hugs from parents help convey to a teenager a sense of security at a time when the rapid changes in personality can make life and identity seem very uncertain.

You are the best sex education your children will get and by far the most important sexual fact you can communicate is the sanctity and delight of your own marriage. Young people need vision, living pictures of how to love, demonstrations that God's way really works. If they can see that the flame of romance burns brightly in your marriage and that faithfulness brings no loss of excitement, they'll know what to look for in their own lives. Instead of rebelling against your values they'll seek to emulate them.

And that kind of propagation is what true parenthood is all about.

A LIFETIME OF LOVE

In this final section we consider some of the common challenges to long-term sexual harmony, together with ways of overcoming them. We also look positively at the effects of the passing years on the enjoyment of love-making.

Long-lasting happiness isn't automatic. As with all precious things love has to be cared for; but, provided you're committed to doing that, there's no reason why you shouldn't experience all the delights which come as the reward of faithfulness.

15

Keep the Home Fires Burning

Most people who marry do so in the hope that they'll be together for the rest of their lives. That proves to be an impossible dream for many. Divorce rates are at an all-time high in the Western world, to such an extent that a lot of young people fear to make the commitment at all rather than face the pain of betrayed trust and dashed hopes.

But it need not be so. With God's help it's perfectly possible to ride the ups and downs of life together and to enjoy a love which grows all the richer for the passing years.

Familiarity doesn't have to breed contempt. It can result in a profound appreciation of your partner's qualities in the same way that a virtuoso violinist discovers the full potential of a Stradivarius by the long experience of playing it. Instead of becoming bored he's for ever excited by the challenge of bringing out the best from his instrument. Not that we're suggesting either of you is a mere instrument in your partner's hands, of course!

If you follow the counsel which we've given in the previous pages you can expect to settle down into a well-adjusted and thoroughly satisfying sex life within quite a short time, say, no more than a year or so. From then onwards love begins its long maturing process. The uncertainty and inexperience of youth gradually gives way to a confident skill as you explore and extend the range of your love-making episodes. Your growing security causes the early inhibitions to fall away so that you become progressively more adventurous in what you do. You learn to pace yourselves perfectly for a simultaneous orgasm virtually every time.

The ensuing years will bring you great happiness, not least as you develop the ability to relish the full flavour of your love. The slight slowing down which comes with time will be well compensated by the growth of a more intense passion for one another. In fact, the high plateau of sexual fulfilment comes for most married women not until their late thirties and early forties, making this an absolutely superb time of life for both partners. By now a sexually awakened wife will often be the initiator in love-making, much to the surprise and delight of her husband, who should certainly not have lost his own fire by that age.

How sad then that so many fail at their marriages and what began in hope now finishes up in the disillusionment of the divorce courts. What a waste of love. It's like asking a Yehudi Menuhin to give up the violin in favour of the penny whistle. No doubt it can be done, but what an unnecessary loss.

Temptations

The pressures on marriage in our society come particularly upon its sexual aspects. Jesus described his day as: 'This adulterous and sinful generation' (Mark 8:38). Nothing has changed. We live in a world full of temptations to marital infidelity, some overtly sexual, others more subtle and complex in the way they seek to destroy love. We have to be aware of the dangers and take positive action to counteract them.

For example, here's a wife at home immersed in the thoroughly noble but nonetheless unglamorous task of raising children. She finds it quite impractical to put on her face and a snazzy dress first thing in the morning while preparing sandwiches, ironing a shirt and scrubbing the children's faces. As her husband leaves for work she's hardly at her best. When he arrives back at 6 p.m.—the lowest time of day for most of us—he finds her harassed with cooking the meal and getting the children ready for bed. Again, she's scarcely looking like the model housewife in the TV adverts.

But the girl at work has no such problems. This same husband sees her walk into his office smartly dressed and well made up. She's pleasant, professional and attractive. At the first sign of the image slipping she retreats to the ladies room to redress the damage. And at the end of the day when even she's beginning to fray at the edges she vanishes into commuterland to reappear on the morrow looking as good as new. It's a bit of an unfair competition, isn't it?

Knowing that no man is invulnerable to the girl who is on the pill and dressed to kill, especially if she takes a fancy to him, what is a wife to do in this sort of situation?

What she mustn't do is get under the pressure to compete. No wife should feel she's got to maintain a glamorous demeanour in the home as though she were one of the girls at work. If that's the case then the marriage is built upon a shaky foundation from the start. But that doesn't mean she's to opt out, either.

It doesn't actually take a lot to keep a loving husband safe. Five minutes in front of the mirror before he arrives home won't make you any less harassed, but at least you won't look it quite so much! Or how about sending him on his way in the morning with something to occupy his wandering moments. You may be in your dressing gown with your hair looking like a haystack after a hurricane when he departs, but slip his hand under that dressing gown to feel your breast as you give him his sandwiches—whisper suggestively, 'See you later, darling,'—and you'll put something in his mind which is fair competition for anyone he might meet during the day.

Periodically remind your husband that you have the power to seduce him whenever you want. You'll never demean yourself by doing so because seduction carries with it the ability to withhold favours as well as offer them. It's a 'come and get me if you can' attitude rather than a pathetic pleading for his affections. You may entice your man with all the passion of a *femme fatale* or with the feigned innocence of a little girl lost, but in this, at least, you're in charge.

You don't need to do this every day; just often enough to act as an antidote to the curlers, face pack and worn-out slippers. That air of mystery, the possibility of the unexpected will do much to protect your husband from temptation. If you're a come hither woman, he's unlikely to wander thither.

Of course, that same harassed housewife is not immune to temptation herself. 'The milkman' may be a bit of a joke, but possibly not the friend, neighbour or tradesman who takes a well-intentioned interest in her.

What is most likely to make a wife vulnerable to the attentions of other men is a combination of loneliness and the feeling that she's being taken for granted. Few women are so naive as to be seduced by good looks or blatant sexual suggestiveness. Nor is the average wife so desperately randy that she's just dying to fall into bed with the first man who offers! It's generally more subtle than that. Picture this scene, for example.

Tania is a good-looking and intelligent thirty-four-year-old mother of three. Two of the children are at school, the other is still a baby. Her husband works long hours and often brings work home. His nightly routine consists largely of complaining about the office over dinner, following which he plonks himself in front of the television for half an hour before getting immersed in a pile of business papers for the rest of the evening. Tania puts the children to bed and does the ironing. They have intercourse briefly twice a week.

There's one bright spark in Tania's life. His name is Michael, the jobbing gardener who comes by once a week. He's of similar age, a pleasant and helpful man who always has time to talk. Over the months, Tania has opened up to him about herself and he seems genuinely to understand her. They have much in common.

One day, he finds her particularly distressed because she's

had a row with her husband. He puts a comforting arm around her and she promptly bursts into tears on his shoulder. Neither realizes at this point just how short is the path to the bedroom. It proves, in fact, to be only a few more steps. Tania and her husband are now divorced.

What is a husband to do? It's obviously not the answer to lock your wife away from all contact with men. She doesn't require a social chastity belt in order to protect her virtue!

What your wife does need is someone who understands her, a person to whom she can talk and express her feelings, even vent her frustrations. That someone is *you*! A good husband is more than a romantic lover and provider for his family, he is also his wife's best friend. This means you must take time to share together as friends do. Good communication is the key to a happy marriage.

Your wife also needs your encouragement and appreciation. Housework and child-raising, as with everything else, can on occasions seem a demanding and thankless task. A few appreciative words can make all the difference—especially if accompanied by flowers, a new dress or an evening out!

All this applies just as much if your wife goes out to work. The added pressure which this so often creates can easily be exploited by an unscrupulous colleague, given half a chance. You need to be even more conscientious about properly communicating, lest you find yourselves living two almost separate lives. Somebody may just decide to step into the gap.

Should either of you ever find the unbelievable is happening and a third party is intruding into your relationship then you must act swiftly. To use James Dobson's phrase, love must be tough. It's no Christian virtue to be 'understanding' if your partner becomes infatuated with someone else. You entered an exclusive lifelong covenant which is binding before God whether you were married in a cathedral, chapel or registry office. Adultery, whether it be of a homosexual kind, gross flirtation or actual intercourse breaks the covenant and provides biblical grounds for divorce. Whatever the reasons, you must confront your partner with the implications of the action and state categorically that you won't tolerate two-timing.

When people become infatuated they lose their sense of reality. Although a firm stand made early on may seem the opposite of what you think you should do, it's actually the right thing. A bucket of cold water will sober a drunk far more effectively than a thousand wheedling words. Call it jealousy if you like, but everyone has the right to be jealous for their own marriage.

Mental adultery

Of course, adultery may remain in the mind. Many people fantasize about making love to someone else, particularly when engaged in sexual intercourse. The origins of these fantasies are various: it may be ideas put there through reading pornography, or lust for someone you know, perhaps the memory of a former relationship, or a famous personality, a girl on the beach. Fantasies are fashioned from what we allow into our minds.

Jesus said, 'I tell you that anyone who looks at a woman lustfully has already committed adultery with her in his heart' (Matthew 5:28). This means that mental adultery is as unacceptable to God as actual adultery—even though the earthly consequences are different.

How are we to handle this common temptation? You can't make love with an empty head so it's no use simply trying to push fantasies out. What's required is something better in their place—wholesome fantasy about your own partner.

One of the values of celebration sex (see chapter 12) is that it provides a store of unusual encounters which your minds can later relive. Romantic memories and remembered words, sexy poses and seductive scenes engraved on the mind will provide ample material for your mental stimulation without the need to trespass beyond the bounds of your own relationship. If you wish you can create your own storylines, erotic tales about yourselves, akin to the Song of Songs. If you're given to a bit of drama you can even enact scenes from your play. We don't think it a good idea to take photos, make videos or write the story down. The trouble is, if your children or friends don't find it, you might just die and have the relatives come across it in the effects! Keep your love tales within the privacy of your own minds.

We consider pornography to be a most unhelpful substitute for what you create for yourselves. Whether in a pictorial or written form, it dehumanizes people and turns sex into a merely animal encounter. Although it may stimulate our sexual mechanisms it has no power to promote love. Lustful provocation will not produce sexual compatibility. The key to that lies in the power of a passionate sacrificial love for one another. The growth of such love isn't aided if while your bodies are engaged in intercourse your minds are committing adultery because of pornographically induced fantasies. From a Christian perspective, that alone makes it unacceptable.

Although pornography may be a temptation to either sex, one of the particular pleasures of life for most men is looking at pretty girls. Many a wife wonders how her husband can claim fidelity to her and at the same time glance at every attractive woman he sees. His behaviour can make her feel very threatened. Christian men often worry about this tendency of their eyes to stray. Is it sinful or just natural?

The power of a woman's body over a man's eyes isn't determined by the relationship alone but by the very form itself. A beautiful woman, any beautiful woman, is attractive to a man. That's how they're made. Which means men have an insatiable curiosity, a fascination to look. As we've said earlier, that originates in the way in which God introduced Adam and Eve to one another.

Any appreciation of beauty in God's creation, including that of women, should produce thanksgiving to God. Sadly, because of the Fall, it usually doesn't. Most men eye girls with lustful thoughts in their minds. So what is a Christian man to do? Job gives us the answer. 'I made a covenant with my eyes not to look lustfully at a girl' (Job 31:1). A marriage covenant is a commitment to have eyes of desire only for your wife.

That's the test, and a man must be faithful to himself in this, let alone to his wife. Does the looking involve lust, the desire to feel, to possess, to fantasize about making love to her? If so, it is sinful. Or does he simply admire God's creation and give thanks?

It's helpful to talk about these matters in the course of your relationship. As a wife you'll best serve your husband not by reacting every time he glances at another woman but by being on his side. Instead of making him feel guilty, be open about it. If you see an attractive girl coming towards you both, say, 'She's pretty, isn't she?' Lust and secrecy go hand in hand. By keeping things in the light like this you'll do much to protect your man from the undoubted temptations which he faces. It will not only do him good to know he can discuss the subject with you, but it will also quell your own suspicions and uncertainties—and that makes for mutual security.

Fatigue

So far we've concentrated upon things which can stimulate our sexual appetites in wrong directions but the vagaries of life may also depress our desire for each other.

High on the list for both sexes must come the demands of work employment. A friend of ours applying for a middle management post was asked at his interview, 'What comes first, your job or your family?' When he replied that it was the latter, they told him he was unsuitable.

This is, of course, bad business practice. A man with a secure home life is going to be a more stable and productive employee than the 'company man'. He's also likely to have significantly better health and be less prone to stress diseases. The same goes for a woman.

In spite of this there's a growing trend to let pressure come upon marriage by demanding long hours, weekend working and attendance at conferences by employees, particularly in the professional sector. It can be even harder for a woman if she faces the unfair additional pressure of having to prove she's just as good as a man at her job by performing better than everyone else.

Matters aren't made any easier if you're in the kind of church whose life consists of a large number of evening meetings, especially if they tend to run late. Add watching a lot of late-night television to all this and you have a major reason for a decline in sexual bliss: sheer tiredness.

Recent research suggests that tiredness in men now ranks alongside the traditional woman's headache as an apology for not wanting to make love. Constant fatigue can easily produce a jaded outlook on life so that the early zeal—the spark—goes out of the relationship. And once sex becomes boring, predictable and unfulfilling the temptation comes to look elsewhere—the seven-year itch, or ten, or fifteen, or twenty....

What's to be done to guard against this happening? Our own way of coping has been periodically to review our lifestyle and rejuvenate it where necessary. We ask ourselves questions like: are we doing too much? Do we think we're indispensable in our jobs? Are we motivated by faith or demand? Is the wrong secular style of living squeezing us into its overstressed mould? Do we need a telly-fast (a week or two with the plug pulled out)? Are we attending meetings with a sense of purpose or because they're in the programme?

We've seldom needed to make radical changes as a result of our review, but a few minor adjustments have often produced a freshness which touches not only our marriage bed but many other aspects of life as well. Considering your ways every so often is a beneficial biblical practice.

Tiredness and lowered sexual vitality often result from physical unfitness. By and large our society is overweight and underexercised, and people are becoming increasingly aware that this is a major cause of ill health and premature death.

Christians have the highest motivation of all for looking after their bodies—they are temples of the Holy Spirit. We're not suggesting you become fanatical or faddish, but a sensible review of your eating habits and the incorporation of some regular exercise into your life can do much to increase your energy reserves for God. And that greatly benefits your love-life. Both of you can benefit from exercising your pelvic-floor muscles in order to keep your sexual apparatus in good tone, in addition to whatever else you might do. Ten squeezes a day, at least.[1]

Impotence

Men don't undergo the change of life in the way that women do, nonetheless many experience some kind of mid-life crisis and this can affect the sexual side of marriage. A man in, say, his mid-forties knows that if he's not made something of his life by now he's unlikely ever to do so. This realization can be quite depressing and produce a sense of failure, a feeling of for ever lost opportunities and a wishing that things had turned out differently. Should a man be made redundant during this period of life he can be quite devastated. Symptoms may vary but could include depression, restlessness, anxiety, insomnia, alcoholism, an attempt at recapturing lost youth by having an affair with a younger woman—and sexual impotence.

A man's inability on occasions to raise the standard, as it were, is a standing joke in our society (if you'll pardon the pun). But for the one experiencing the problem it may be shameful and shattering. He's no longer man enough to please his wife.

Mid-life crisis is far from being the only cause of sexual impotence. Diabetes, alcoholism, taking anti-depressants, tiredness and general illness can all affect a man's ability to

[1] For a fuller discussion of the matter of healthy living, see John Houghton, *The Healthy Alternative* (Kingsway Publications 1985).

achieve or sustain an erection. But the most common reasons are psychological rather than physical.

Significant impotence occurring early in marriage may have its roots in a dominant mother/weak father syndrome. This can produce a subconscious aversion to women in general, sometimes leading to homosexuality. Or, if such a man marries a strong-willed wife, he may feel overwhelmed and inadequate, and this makes him impotent. The key to avoiding this is to follow the biblical pattern for family life as expressed in Ephesians 5:21–6:4.

A man may fear sexual failure because he takes a long time to reach a climax. His anxiety can induce impotence. That fear may have begun in a rushed encounter with a prostitute, or in his wife always wanting to get it over and done with quickly because she was herself uninterested or worried about being overheard. Living under the same roof as parents during early marriage is a particularly bad idea in this respect.

Another source of impotence is a neglect of talking through life's problems together. A man's physical failure may be an unconscious attempt at gaining his wife's attention. If she doesn't then respond he may go off her completely, using his impotence as a form of punishment against her. 'You don't want me, so you won't have my body either.'

Virtually all men experience impotence at some time during the course of their marriage. It's usually on isolated occasions and brought about by obvious factors like tiredness and overwork. It's unlikely to last more than two or three days and is easily overcome. If it lasts longer or is accompanied by significant mood changes then it needs taking seriously. A review of your lifestyle, a medical check-up, a holiday and maybe some professional counsel is called for.

The secret of overcoming impotence lies with a wife. She mustn't overreact and start crying, 'It's all my fault. I've lost my looks. I'm no longer any good in bed.' Nor, of course, must she laugh at her husband or, even worse, criticize him for his non-performance. That's the easiest way to make it a permanent condition.

On those odd occasions when it happens through sheer exhaustion the best thing you can do is smile sweetly, cuddle him close and say, 'Never mind, darling. You know I love you. We'll try again tomorrow when you're less tired.' If he can see the wryness of the situation and laugh at it, there's no reason why you shouldn't laugh together. There's plenty of room for jokes like, '*Wilt* thou take this woman?' 'I wilt.' 'I know!' if he's in that frame of mind. The important thing is to boost his confidence again. The right kind of humour often does that.

Should it be a bit more serious, apart from taking sensible steps to sort life out together, you shouldn't attempt intercourse for a few days, say seven to ten, but simply enjoy fondling one another. You can then try the wife-on-top position. If it works, well and good. If not, return to caressing each other. What you mustn't do is give up in despair. It's a mistake to let your sex life peter out in mid-life because of difficulties which, in the event, may well prove to be only temporary.

By no means all men undergo a mid-life crisis and those who do may not necessarily become impotent. Certainly you shouldn't look to the future with grim foreboding. If you attain a good sexual adjustment early in your marriage, if you communicate well and if you keep a regular eye on your lifestyle, all will be well. We know of many wonderful, long-lasting marriages in which the partners have kept faithful to each other through all the temptations and have enjoyed an exhilarating uninterrupted life of love-making. If you keep stoking the fire and shake out the ash every so often there's no reason at all why the flame should ever go out.

As we've focused somewhat on the problems which beset men in the latter part of this chapter, in the next we'll look at a challenge which sooner or later confronts every married woman.

16

The Change of Life

If all has gone well, by the time you reach your forties you'll be a very experienced woman sexually. Not only will you have made love to your husband many hundreds of times but you'll have learned most of the tricks in the book. You'll know exactly how to turn him on and what pleases him most. With your own sexuality now fully ripened you'll be enjoying the most superb satisfaction yourself.

Such experience should make you a very confident and secure woman. You are a successful lover. The beloved in the Song of Songs captures this sense of sexual maturity when she sings, 'I am a wall, and my breasts are like towers. Thus I have become in his eyes like one bringing contentment' (Song of Songs 8:10). Happy is the man with such a woman!

This confidence can be threatened by the onset of the menopause, or change of life. Misunderstanding about what's happening, coupled with negative thinking, may make a woman feel that even if she weathers the storm, nothing will be the same afterwards. All that she's built has been torn down in a matter of months; suddenly she's old and must resign herself to the fact. Sexually she's rapidly become a dried-out prune.

Nothing could be further from the truth. Life and love are far from over. We want to suggest a much more positive approach to the situation when it arises and we'll begin that by explaining what really takes place.

The menopause commences commonly between the ages of forty-five and fifty years. The precise time is determined by all kinds of factors, such as hereditary traits, when you reached puberty, even at what altitude you live, and so forth. There are no hard and fast rules. It could occur as early as forty or as late as fifty-five.

The first sign of its onset is erratic periods. You may find one month the flow is scant, the next copious. Cycles get longer but become unpredictable. You begin to miss periods or get two in a month. Gradually they cease altogether.

This is brought about by a marked drop in oestrogen production, with the result that eggs no longer ripen in your ovaries. So your womb ceases to prepare for the possibility of conception. It's all part of the wisdom of God, because bearing children is beyond the physical capacity of old women. If there were no menopause we'd have eighty-year-old mums-to-be sitting in the ante-natal clinic!

The hormone balance in our bodies is quite fine and sudden changes can have a dramatic effect on both our moods and the way in which we function. Hence, the drop in oestrogen production, coupled with other hormonal fluctuations, can produce some discomforting symptoms.

The most commonly reported symptom is the hot flush, but menopausal women may also complain of fatigue, night sweats, headaches, insomnia, depression and irritability. Some experience palpitations, dizzy spells and a crawling feeling on the skin. Obviously these symptoms contribute to one another; for example, a night sweat which makes you throw the bedclothes off only then to get freezing cold, will break your sleep and cause tiredness. You might also catch a chill. Many of these symptoms are amplifications of those which you may experience just before your periods.

Hot flushes can be particularly irritating because they make you look as though you're blushing and you may feel that it's a kind of public announcement that you're going through the change of life. Not too helpful for your self-image. But for all that it's better not to avoid company.

If the symptoms are severe you can obtain hormone replacement therapy (HRT) from your doctor. This consists of pills to supplement your body's natural supplies. However, medical opinion is divided as to the value or wisdom of such therapy, and many would advocate riding the storm out and letting things take their natural course as the best way of coping.

How we handle any change in our lives is largely determined by our character and our relationships. A woman whose identity has been superficially built upon her ability to remain poised and restrained in company may have more difficulty than one with a more relaxed reputation. The highly strung and overintense, or the desperately unfulfilled are likely also to encounter problems. There's much to be said for letting God sort out our major personality defects early in life!

Proverbs 17:22 says, 'A cheerful heart is good medicine, but a crushed spirit dries up the bones.' If you've developed an optimistic outlook and can recognize this as a temporary phase which doesn't mean the end of your active life, you'll come through successfully. And it does have its advantages. No more contraceptives—and no more periods!

It's important to understand that the cessation of your childbearing ability doesn't mean a loss of femininity. You continue to produce the hormones which make you a woman. Nor do you lose your sexual drive. That store of experience is not all swept away by the menopause. You can carry on enjoying sexual intercourse for many happy years to come; you're simply not past it at fifty.

Although there will be moments when you feel especially delicate, we recommend that by and large you make this an active period of life. Keep involved with younger people as well as those of your own age. As an experienced wife you have much to pass on to those new to marriage. In fact, it's a biblical responsibility to do so (see Titus 2:3–5). Dress well, get out and about, pay some attention to your health and general fitness, take up a sport if necessary. And continue to make love with enthusiasm.

As far as that is concerned it's generally advised that you should continue to use contraceptives for two years after your last period if you're below fifty and for one year if you're over fifty.

It's possible that you'll produce less vaginal lubrication than you used to but that can easily be overcome by supplementing it with saliva, oil or gel when you make love. The reduction in oestrogen production causes your reproductive organs gradually to shrink and the vaginal walls to thin somewhat. This can make intercourse painful without adequate lubrication. You may also be able to obtain a hormone cream from your doctor if you do suffer any discomfort.

Keeping close to your husband is essential at this time. He more than anyone else can support you with sympathy, tenderness and encouragement. You'll be fine if he's learned the art of romance and knows how to make you feel young and attractive. Make sure he gets plenty of practice beforehand!

Each phase of our lives has its blessings as well as its problems. The secret of successful living lies in recognizing those blessings and using them to overcome the difficulties. Mid-life may include the menopause, but it's also a time when you've gained a lot of insight into the meaning of life. You care much less about people's opinions of you. And you have an ability to savour all that's best about life and love.

There's a special promise given to those who know God:

> The righteous will flourish like a palm tree, they will grow like a cedar of Lebanon; planted in the house of the Lord, they will flourish in the courts of our God. They will still bear fruit in old age, they will stay fresh and green (Psalm 92:12–14).

In other words, you'll be a ripe plum—not a dried-up old prune!

But more of that in the next chapter.

17

Retirement, Never!

There's much truth in the saying: 'You're as old as you feel.'
Folk with a youthful outlook tend to live healthier and more
active lives in their later years than those who resign themselves to being old and act accordingly.

Sadly, there are people who not only consider sex is just for
the younger generation but who convince themselves that
they are too old for it in any case. If you think like that it's more
than likely that your love-life will draw to a close long before
your days are ended. This will produce frustration and tension
in your relationship just when one hopes that a lifetime of
love will be crowned with the mellow glory of fully matured
love-making. Whether your retirement years are golden or
grey will depend in large measure upon what kind of outlook
you have and how you regard the long-term future of your
love-life. So, what are the sexual prospects for your later
years?

As a husband you'll experience a steadier ageing process
than your wife in the sense that there's no physical equivalent
to the menopause. You'll produce less sperm as the years
progress, but in all likelihood you will still be capable of
fathering a child well into your seventies. Not that you'll
probably want to! When you're about sixty years of age your
production of the male hormone, testosterone, will settle to a
level which is adequate enough to maintain your sexual

166

desire for your wife. Some hardening of the blood vessels may make it a little more difficult to obtain an erection than when you were younger but, by the same token, it's likely to stay up longer. You'll certainly still be capable of intercourse.

As you know, it takes some time for a man to attain another erection after he's ejaculated. When you're young that can be quite brief. As you age this period lengthens until in old age it could be as much as several days. However, if you have intercourse without ejaculating every time—as is sometimes desirable in later life—you'll remain capable of achieving a more frequent erection. This will allow you still to make love with reasonable frequency and to meet your wife's needs.

Of course, the later years of life do tend to bring their share of health problems. Some men experience an enlargement of their prostate gland. This betrays itself by pain and difficulty upon urinating, especially starting and stopping, along with a general ache in the pelvic region. There may also be a burning sensation in the bladder and pain at the tip of the penis. (Incidentally, the fact that as a younger man you may on occasions have difficulty in passing water after, say, a long drive doesn't mean you've got prostate trouble.)

Sometimes an enlarged prostate gland is surgically removed. This doesn't leave you impotent. You'll still be capable of intercourse and orgasm though you won't actually ejaculate any longer.

Men are more prone to heart attacks than women in our society. That risk can be greatly reduced by attention to your health in earlier years. In particular, keeping the weight down, not smoking, being moderate with alcohol, taking adequate exercise and learning to relax will significantly help. But even should you have a heart attack the consensus of medical opinion is that it probably does more good to resume sexual relations afterwards than to avoid intercourse for fear of another attack.

As a wife, once you've come through the throes of the menopause your hormones will readjust so that you still remain very much a woman. Although, as with your husband, sexual arousal may take longer as the years progress, none-theless you'll still be quite capable of enjoying intercourse and reaching orgasm.

There's no need for you to lose your sense of confidence as a sexually desirable woman in spite of the fact that your looks won't be those of a twenty-year-old. You'll have something you didn't have then: a lifetime's experience of sexual passion which still burns strong even though the house is looking a bit worn. As the elderly white-haired wife said, 'The fact that there's snow on the roof doesn't mean the fire's gone out in the grate!'

There are two health worries which especially concern women. One is breast cancer and the other is cancer of the cervix. In both cases, if the problem is noticed early enough, drastic surgery, let alone death, can often be avoided.

Every woman should regularly check her own breasts for lumps or discharge. We've included the standard procedure in Appendix Two. Even if you do find a lump it may well be a benign cyst or a swollen lymph gland, but you should still check it out with your doctor as soon as possible. The quicker you do this the less likelihood there is of needing the total removal of a breast should the lump be cancerous.

It's a very open question as to whether a woman's thinking can affect her chances of contracting cancer, but in view of the fact that we're becoming increasingly aware of the rela-tionship between mental outlook and health we do feel it important that you always accept and love your own breasts, particularly as you get older and they become less firm and shapely. We trust that your husband will still appreciate their charms, too. Breastfeeding is known to reduce the risk of cancer as well. In other words, instead of regretting these appendages, as some women do, use them for their God-given purpose of feeding babies and for ever attracting your husband. We suspect this may enhance your resistance to disease.

Cancer of the cervix (see under Appendix One) and other troubles such as fibroids can all be detected in their early treatable stages if you periodically book a screening at your local women's clinic, Family Planning Clinic or GP's Health Centre. Once every three years is sufficient. A simple, painless smear test, that is, a sample of cervical mucus is examined for tell-tale signs. The resultant peace of mind is well worth the little effort.

Even if you are unfortunate enough to require a hysterectomy, that is, removal of all or part of your womb, it doesn't mean the end of your sex life. Your vagina won't be taken away, nor your ovaries. In any case, drastic surgery is gradually being replaced by increasingly effective drug treatments.

Old age isn't a disease but a time of maturity; your later years are for enjoying the full flowering of a lifetime romance. You'll possess many fond memories of your shared life, coupled with a deep trust and understanding of one another which, God willing, will last for many years. There's every reason to expect that you'll still manage and enjoy intercourse as often as you wish into ripe old age. And even if at times you do feel too tired for it, you'll never be past love. At a more leisurely pace you'll still be able to comfort and caress one another, to speak your words of affection and share the riches of your companionship.

Of course, one day it must end; we marry until we are separated by death. Unless you both die at once, one of you will experience bereavement.

Such thoughts are horrific when you're young. The last thing you want to think about is death. And that's fair enough. God wants us to enjoy what we've got without for ever glancing over our shoulders in anticipation of some fearful doom. At the same time, it does us no harm to recognize that all good things must come to an end. From a Christian point of view, that's no cause for despair; our hope always extends beyond the grave. Death may mark the end of our earthly love but it's also the doorway into the full enjoyment of God's eternal love.

And one day, at the end of time, we shall understand that even our love as husbands and wives was just the reflection of a greater love between Christ and his church. The present age sees only the engagement; the new age will dawn with the unveiling of the church in all her splendour for her marriage to Jesus, the Lamb of God.

> I saw the Holy City, the new Jerusalem, coming down out of heaven from God, prepared as a bride beautifully dressed for her husband.... 'There will be no more death or mourning or crying or pain, for the old order of things has passed away.... I am making everything new!' (Revelation 21:2, 4–5).

In the meantime, we hope you'll enjoy to the full this superb gift of sexual pleasure for many happy years and prove for yourselves that it is so much more than *just* a touch of love.

APPENDICES

Sexually Transmitted Diseases

Most at risk are those who have had sexual intercourse with a number of partners, though a disease may occur after just one encounter with an infected person.

Early treatment is vital, especially with the more serious complaints. Don't neglect any symptoms which you have or have had in the past, particularly those relating to syphilis or gonorrhoea. These do not get better by themselves even though the symptoms disappear. If you are in any doubt go to your GP or a Special Clinic (see telephone directory under Venereal Diseases) as soon as possible.

AIDS

Acquired Immune Deficiency Syndrome is a serious and often fatal condition produced by a retrovirus which interferes with the patient's ability to resist disease. As a consequence the victim contracts a large number of illnesses and it is the cumulative effect of these which may lead to death.

The virus is transmitted via blood, for example, through breaks in the skin. As anal intercourse often produces some damage to the mucous membranes the disease has spread especially among homosexuals, though it is by no means confined to them. Women may contract it, as may intravenous drug abusers of either sex.

At present treatment is confined to dealing with the various infections as no cure for AIDS has been found.

Cervical cancer

The theory that male circumcision protected a woman against developing cervical cancer has now been discredited. It is today generally recognized that the major cause of the disease is a woman having multiple sexual partners, especially if she starts young and if she contracts herpes or warts virus infections. One possibility is that the cervix develops immunity to the first semen it encounters but not to that of subsequent men. Hence, a woman who has only one 'clean' partner becomes 'one-flesh' with him and is safe; but a promiscuous woman is at risk.

Cervical smear tests can give early warning of cancer so that preventative treatment can be administered in good time. A woman at risk or who has been at risk should have regular three-year tests.

Crabs

Crab lice are mites which infest the pubic hair and produce itching in the genital area. Treatment is with gamma BHC lotion.

Cystitis

A scalding pain on passing water, coupled with an inability to hold it for long even though there is hardly any to pass, is usually indicative of cystitis. Other symptoms may be feverishness, pain in the lower back or abdomen and cloudy or blood-flecked urine. The cause is commonly bacteria getting into the urethra and bladder where they multiply rapidly. However, the symptoms are sometimes caused by allergies to toiletries, anxiety, depression or irritation produced by sexual intercourse. More seriously, other sexually transmitted diseases may be responsible for the symptoms.

Self-help consists of drinking as much water as possible (see chapter 7), resting in the warm with hot water bottles, taking some bicarbonate of soda and a couple of mild pain-killers. However, if the symptoms do not clear within a day or so, or you have cause to suspect something more, then medical treatment should be sought. See Appendix Five for helpful literature.

Genital warts

From one to six months after infective intercourse this virus produces groups of warts, often in small clusters, on the genitals or around the anus. As with ordinary warts, they can be treated surgically or with caustic paints.

Gonorrhoea

The first symptoms in men are a burning pain on passing urine and a greenish discharge from the penis with sometimes swollen glands in the groin. If neglected the disease may spread to other parts of the reproductive apparatus causing urine retention and severely painful, swollen testicles. The latter can lead to permanent sterility.

Women experience the same burning sensation on passing urine. The vulva is red and raw and there is vaginal discharge. If the disease spreads as far as the Fallopian tubes permanent sterility will follow. However, it should be noted that some strains of gonorrhoea produce virtually no symptoms in women. The disease can then be unintentionally passed on to a partner and affect the eyes of a new-born baby.

Treatment usually consists of one large injection of procaine penicillin, but some strains are resistant and various other antibiotics may have to be tried.

Herpes

Genital herpes is caused by a virus related to the one which produces cold sores around the mouth. Itchy blisters form on the genitals which then burst leaving painful, shallow ulcers. There may be some feverishness. The symptoms pass within two weeks but can keep reoccurring.

There is no certain cure at present.

Non-specific urethritis

NSU is a widespread complaint caused by any number of organisms, notably chlamydia trachomatis. After an incubation period of up to three months, but often within one month, symptoms similar to those of gonorrhoea develop, that is, painful urination and discharge. There may also be abdominal pain and sometimes acute arthritis.

Treatment is with antibiotics though the symptoms may be recurrent.

Syphilis

This serious disease has three stages:

1. A painless sore (chancre) appears at the point of infection ten to forty days after the disease is contracted. This may be on the clitoris, vulva, cervix (where it can be missed), anus, nipple, mouth, penile head or foreskin. It is a hard red pimple up to 1cm in diameter which grows moist and eroded then vanishes within four to ten weeks. The body is already invaded with germs.

2. A skin rash appears and patches of hair drop out anytime between one-and-a-half and three months. Swollen glands, sore throat, headache and feverishness may accompany this. Within a year all symptoms will have vanished as the disease becomes dormant.

3. As much as thirty years later the disease will revive and attack the body indiscriminately, forming tumours and

damaging the heart, circulation, brain, spinal cord, bones, ligaments and skin. Blindness, paralysis, insanity and death are likely. The damage is irreversible.

Syphilis can be effectively treated in the early stages by means of a ten-day course of procaine penicillin injections.

Thrush

Thrush or candida is not usually a sexually transmitted disease but is caused by a naturally occurring yeast-like organism multiplying too much. Diabetics are prone to this because of excess blood sugar, as are those who are obese or who wear poorly ventilated underclothing which provides the conditions for rapid growth of the fungus. It is also a common complaint arising from the use of antibiotics.

Symptoms are an itchy swollen vulva and a curdy white vaginal discharge. Intercourse and urination are painful. Men may develop a red spotty penis, especially under the foreskin.

Treatment is with Nystatin. See Appendix Five for useful literature.

Trichomoniasis

This is caused by a microscopic parasite which produces a foul-smelling, green, frothy discharge. The vulva and vagina become inflamed. Men are seldom affected but may carry the parasite.

Treatment consists of a course of Flagyl tablets.

Examining Your Breasts

Every woman should develop the habit of regularly checking that her breasts are healthy. The best time to examine them is once a month just after your period when they're usually at their softest. If your periods have ceased, do so on the first day of the month, so that you remember it.

Breast inspection involves both *looking* and *feeling*.

Looking

Undress to the waist then stand before a mirror in good light with your arms hanging loosely by your sides. Get to know the normal appearance of your breasts. No two are the same; one is usually slightly larger and one somewhat lower than the other.

You should, on subsequent examinations, look for:

—any change in the size or shape of either breast.
—any swelling, rash, dimpling, puckering or discolouration of the skin.
—any unusually prominent veins.
—any turning in on itself, or distortion of either nipple.
—any bleeding or discharge from either nipple when you squeeze them.

You should observe your breasts from all angles by turning from side to side, not forgetting to look underneath as well.

Repeat this examination:
—with your hands placed lightly on your head, elbows out.
—with your arms stretched straight above your head.
—with your hands on your hips and pressing inwards until you feel your chest muscles tighten.

Feeling

Lie on the bed with your head on a pillow. Place a folded towel under the shoulder of the side you wish to examine first. Use the opposite hand to do the feeling and place the hand you're not using under your head. You'll have to get used to the feel of your own breasts. Many women have quite lumpy ones, particularly just prior to their periods, but often all month. Your object is to check for anything *unusual*.

Use the pads of your fingers, not the tips, and keep them together. Beginning at the nipple, work outwards following a spiral pattern, feeling every part of your breast. Use a gentle but firm pressure against your ribcage. The spiral should extend all the way up to your collar-bone and should include an examination of your armpit and all the way down the side of your breast. Repeat the spiral, only this time with your free arm by your side. Note any unusual lump or thickening. You must not rush or skimp this inspection.

The same process should be repeated on your other breast.

Should you find anything out of the ordinary you should report it to your doctor within the next few days. Most lumps are not cancerous, just harmless cysts, but only a proper medical diagnosis can determine this. Don't let fear put you off reporting anything amiss. Cancer can be treated very successfully if it's caught in the early stages. Promptness in doing so could save your breast—or even your life.

Excellent leaflets have been produced by the Health Education Council and the Women's Cancer Control Campaign and are available from your local health centre. (See Appendix Five.)

The Song of Songs

Sometimes called the Song of Solomon (from the opening verse), this book has been the subject of diverse interpretations. In view of the line which we have taken we feel a word of explanation is called for.

Many commentators have treated the book as an allegory by which they mean that the text is merely the vehicle for a higher, spiritual message. The job of the commentator is to explain this 'hidden meaning' to the reader.

Although the allegorical approach has produced some deeply devotional writings, particularly concerning the believer's love relationship with Christ, it does present grave problems. There is the difficulty of actually agreeing upon the hidden meaning of the verses. In addition, it is questionable whether we should ever ignore the plain literal meaning of Scripture in favour of an almost mystical interpretation. Most serious of all is the fact that the allegorical approach reflects an unbiblical Greek view of the world in which the physical and in particular the sexual is seen as essentially unspiritual. The Bible makes no such sacred/secular divide but sees the whole cosmos as created by God, ruled by God and in the process of being redeemed by God. Physical love in the context of marriage is holy in his sight.

Another popular approach to the Song has been to recognize the reality of the events and the storyline but to claim that the overriding purpose of the book is to convey an added dimension, namely the love of Christ for his church. Hence, most commentators who adopt this line effectively ignore the immediate meaning and concentrate upon this added dimension.

The major problem with this approach is making everything fit. Incredible mental gymnastics are required to make each verse carry a double meaning of this kind. In the end one finishes up with a strained interpretation and, practically speaking, the possibility of preaching upon only a few verses.

All these problems are solved if we read the Song as a love poem, similar in literary style to many others of the era, deliberately placed in Scripture by God to convey and extol the joy of sexual love between a husband and wife. It is the positive to the many negative warnings about adultery and fornication in the Bible. We suspect that, historically, Christians would have appeared better balanced in their views on sex if more had read the text in this way. For this book thoroughly fuses unabashed sexuality with full-blooded romantic love, and does so in the context of uncompromising marital fidelity. That has always been God's will and is never more needing to be heard than in the present day.

Because the poem speaks in such terms it conveys its own meaning and there is no need to look for hidden interpretations, beyond recognizing the fairly obvious *double-entendres* which are used to describe some of the intimacies of lovemaking. This doesn't mean one cannot ever use the story to illustrate the love of Christ and the church. In the same way that Paul in Ephesians 5 parallels the man/woman relationship with that of Christ and the church it is perfectly legitimate to draw some comparisons. But that is quite different from claiming that this is the prime purpose for the existence of the book.

The Song of Songs teaches us the beauty, joy and freshness of human love when expressed in the will of God; it conveys a spirit of sexual celebration. There can be no better antidote than this to the selfishness and cynicism of our society about love and marriage. We hope we have been able to convey something of that spirit of the Song through what we have written.

For those readers who wish to explore this theme further we heartily recommend G. Lloyd Carr's commentary in the IVP Tyndale series.

Guilt Arising from Sexual Abuse

The sexual abuse of children, particularly of girls, is a deplorably common occurrence in our society. Incidents range from illicit fondling by a relative through to forcible rape by a stranger.

Though some girls are able to shrug the event off in a matter-of-fact manner, many are deeply wounded as a result. Often this doesn't fully reveal itself until the girl marries and then discovers that she cannot enjoy sexual relations with her husband without a sense of guilt, shame and uncleanness. This may well leave her frigid, or even anti-sex altogether to the point where the marriage is put at risk. If the assault has been violent she may also suffer from vaginismus (see p.101).

The source of these feelings is two-fold:

1. The plain association of sex with unpleasant memories, especially if the incident involved pain or was sordid and cloaked in secrecy.

2. A misplaced sense of guilt brought on by the reaction of parents or other authority figures. 'What have you been up to?' 'You naughty girl.' 'You must've led him on.' 'I'll kill him when I see him.' 'You know this will have to be reported to the police, don't you?' and so on. Because a young girl is ill-equipped to understand what she is supposed to have done wrong, she can only feel guilty *in general*. It's this undefined sense of disgrace which later colours her attitude

towards sex in adult life. The resultant difficulties can be extremely distressing for a couple who love one another but are unable to experience joy in the bedroom.

We would strongly advise any couple with this problem to seek out some good Christian counsel. However, because that isn't always available we've listed in brief a few of the main points which should be prayerfully considered by those requiring help in this area.

1. The blame needs putting where it belongs. No woman should feel guilty because her body proved attractive to a man or for the molestation which took place. Only if she *deliberately* led the man on should she feel any sense of responsibility, but the weight of guilt rests on the adult who perpetrated the deed. If there is any cause for the woman to feel she has sinned then that sin should be confessed and forgotten. Jesus died to deal absolutely with our sins; the accounts were settled and closed at Calvary (see 1 John 1:9).

2. Forgiving from the heart the one who committed the assault is the key to ending the torment. This forgiveness must be not only for the act itself but for all the subsequent suffering (see Matthew 18:21–35).

3. It's important to recognize that, though capable of abuse, sex is a good gift from God. A woman needs to accept her own body and sexuality as a blessing, not a curse.

4. The woman's husband is God's provision to restore the beauty and purity of that gift to her. It's not true to say, 'All men are the same, they're only after one thing.' *This* man truly loves her and wants to bless her.

5. As a new creation in Christ no believer needs to feel bound by the past (see 2 Corinthians 5:17).

6. The event needs putting in perspective so that it doesn't dominate life. We experience many pains in childhood. Teething pain doesn't stop us enjoying food. Grazed knees don't stop us walking. And childhood sexual trauma, though much more serious, mustn't be allowed to ruin a woman's sex life. She must consciously decide not to be bound by it.

7. Secrecy creates bondage. It's important that the whole

matter is shared through with the husband so that at least one other person knows everything about it (see 1 John 1:7).

8. There needs to be prayer for healing of the emotional damage. This doesn't require any special 'healing of the memories' technique. God delights to heal all who ask him, however they ask.

9. The couple should pray for the Holy Spirit to be present when they make love so that he will bless their union with his own joy and wholesomeness.

Literature Which We Found Useful

Carr, G. Lloyd, *The Song of Solomon* (IVP, 1984).

Dillow, Joseph C. *Solomon on Sex* (Thomas Nelson, 1977).

Eichenlaub, John E. *The Marriage Art* (Mayflower Dell, 1961).

Gardner, R. F. R. *Abortion* (Paternoster Press, 1972).

Guillebaud, John, *The Pill* (OUP, 1984).

Health Education Council, Leaflets: *Cystitis and what to do about it! A self-help guide to thrush, Love-making and hygiene, A guide to examining your breasts, The change of life.*

HMSO *Handbook of Contraceptive Practice* (1984).

LaHaye, Tim & Beverly, *The Act of Marriage* (Zondervan, 1976).

Long, Maureen, *Birthright* (Triangle, 1985).

Lowther, Gail, *Family Planning* (Triangle, 1985).

Miles, Herbert J. *Sexual Happiness in Marriage* (Zondervan, 1967).

Noble, John, *Hide and Sex* (Kingsway, 1981).

Schaeffer, Francis, & C. Everett Koop, *Whatever Happened to the Human Race?* (Marshall, Morgan & Scott, 1980).

Smedes, Lewis, *Sex in the Real World* (Lion, 1979).

Stott, John, *Issues Facing Christians Today* (Marshall, Morgan & Scott, 1984).

The Diagram Group, *Sex: A User's Manual* (Coronet, 1983).

Tomczak, Larry, *Straightforward* (Logos, 1978).

Trobisch, Walter, *I Married You* (IVP, 1971).

Wheat, Ed & Gaye, *Intended for Pleasure* (Scripture Union, 1979).

White, John, *Eros Defiled* (IVP, 1977).

Women's National Cancer Control Campaign, Leaflets: *Your life in your hands, Everyone's doing the breast test.*

Index

Marriage As God Intended

by Selwyn Hughes

'We have never had an argument in the whole of our marriage,' said the husband.
'How did you accomplish that?' asked the counsellor.
'We just don't talk.'

Communication is only one of the problem areas faced by married couples—there can be many other difficulties that cause us to fall short of God's perfect plan.

This book offers help—not only with specific problems, but for improving what is already good and healthy.

There are chapters on:
> relationships with parents and in-laws
> who's the head of the family?
> sexual difficulties
> the temptation to adultery
> divorce and remarriage

Selwyn Hughes is highly respected as a leading marriage guidance counsellor. Here he draws on his many years' experience as both husband and counsellor, blending biblical principles with practical suggestions on how to let God keep your marriage at its best.

 Kingsway Publications